THE COMPLETE POETRY OF

Michelangelo

By Sidney Alexander

NOVELS

Nicodemus
The Hand of Michelangelo
Michelangelo the Florentine
The Celluloid Asylum

BIOGRAPHY

Marc Chagall

HISTORY

Guicciardini's History of Italy
Lions and Foxes

POETRY

The Marine Cemetery:
(Variation on Valéry)
Tightrope in the Dark
Man on the Queue

PLAYS

Salem Story
The Third Great Fool

TRANSLATION

The Berenson Collection
(with Frances Alexander)
The Complete Poetry
of Michelangelo

The Complete Poetry of
Michelangelo

TRANSLATED,

WITH INTRODUCTION

AND NOTES BY

Sidney Alexander

Ohio University Press

ATHENS

Library of Congress Cataloging-in-Publication Data

Michelangelo Buonarroti, 1475–1564
  [Poems, English]
  The complete poetry of Michelangelo / translated with introduction
and notes by Sidney Alexander.
    p. cm.
  ISBN 0-8214-1000-8 (cloth)   0-8214-1049-0 (paper)
  I. Alexander, Sidney, 1912- . II. Title
  PQ4615.B6A66 1991
  851'.4--dc20   91-16240
                                                         CIP

    99 98 97 96 95 94 93 92 5 4 3 2 1 (cloth)
    99 98 97 96 95 94 93   5 4 3 2 1 (paper)

Cover: Michelangelo in the guise of the pessimist philosopher
Heraclitus in Raphael's School of Athens fresco in the Vatican.
Courtesy of Archivi Alinari.

DESIGNED BY LAURY A. EGAN

For

FRANCES

Tu sai che io so, Signora mia, che tu sai . . .

David with the sling
and I with the bow

MICHELAGNIOLO

Written on a manuscript in the Louvre dated 1501–02, containing two sketches for a David, probably the bronze for Pierre de Rohan (disappeared) and a study for the right arm of the marble David (terminated 1504).

The image of the *arco* might very well have been derived from the sculptor's bow, fitted with a bore, used in the Renaissance as a drill: the implication being: I will conquer in my art as David conquered in his.

Also on the drawing in Michelangelo's elegant youthful calligraphy is the first line of sonnet 269 by Petrarch. On the reverse, several other fragmentary Petrarchian-like lines.

'He Speaks Things'

Who is not familiar with Michelangelo Buonarroti: sculptor, painter, architect? But that the titanic Tuscan also possessed (and deserved) a fourth crown of laurel is not sufficiently realized, not even, sadly enough, in his native Florence. His tomb in Santa Croce, designed by Vasari, symbolizes his achievements in the visual arts only: the figure of Poetry is lacking. In the secondary schools, students will read the famous bitter response of Michelangelo to Giovanni Strozzi's verses on the statue of "Night" in the Medici tombs; or they will study the magnificent sonnet beginning "*Non ha l'ottimo artista . . .*" and that is all. But that Michelangelo was the greatest Italian lyrical poet of the sixteenth century is recognized only by specialists in cinquecento literature. What has happened, of course, is best explained in Mark Twain's irritable comment that in Italy whatever was not created by God was created by Michelangelo. A genius so Protean is best acknowledged by ignoring it.

Michelangelo himself refused to take seriously the verses which (especially from his sixtieth year on) he was forever scribbling and revising on the backs of letters, on sheets of drawings, or any other odd scraps of paper at hand. The numerous variants, however, reveal a serious poetic vocation, although the Master liked to call his verses "*polizini*" — "pawntickets" — and often sent his poems to his humanist friends to "fix them up." After all, he was not the only artist of his day who wrote poetry. Everybody in the Renaissance seemed to be doing everything: Cellini committed bad verses as well as murders. Raphael was a city planner who wrote sugary sonnets in which he longed to be imprisoned in the soft chains of his lady's arms. Pope Julius II marched at the head of his troops in military campaigns. The Renaissance ideal was *l'uomo universale*, not an ear and nose specialist.

So the fact that Michelangelo wrote poetry is not surprising. What is surprising is the extraordinary quality of the best of this work. His contemporaries recognized it: the poems circulated in manuscript: a number of madrigals were set to music by celebrated Italian and foreign composers, including Jakob Arcadelt; and in 1546 the humanist Benedetto Varchi lectured on one of Michelangelo's sonnets before the Academy of Florence. The artist was even persuaded to gather together a selection of his verses for publication. The unforeseen death of his friend, the banker, Luigi del Riccio, who had been the patron of such a collection, dissuaded the artist from continuing the project. As it turned out, the poems were not published until 1623, in a corrupt edition misedited by Michelangelo's grandnephew. Fearful for his great ancestor's reputation, the younger Michelangelo committed mayhem on the text, transposing masculine and feminine gender, making elegant what was rough, rewriting images. Not until Cesare Guasti's great edition of 1863 did a responsible text appear.

The poetic works comprise some three hundred pieces, between finished and unfinished. Among the finished pieces there are eighty sonnets, one hundred madrigals, four *capitoli* in *terza-rima*, two sestinas, fifty epitaphs for Cecchino Bracci. The bulk of the verses seem to be the musings of an old man, although some love poems, full of conventional mannerisms, probably are earlier. Michelangelo was particularly fond of the sonnet: within its small space, as within a constricted block of marble, he hammered out harsh Dantesque lines that profoundly express his agony of spirit, now and again lightened by bursts of rough humor. Recurrent themes are the war of himself against himself; repentance for a nameless guilt; art as a symbol of the relationship of God to man; exalted Platonic love, sometimes addressed to Tommaso Cavalieri, more often to Vittoria Colonna; and a religious exaltation of death as liberation.

Despite frequent obscurities and abstract knotted metaphors, Michelangelo's poetry is striking for its ultimate confessional power, a nakedness of soul akin to his nudes in the visual arts. "Be silent! Enough of pallid violets and liquid crystals and sleek beasts," the poet Francesco Berni, a contemporary of Michelangelo, cries out in exasperation against the facile Petrarchian warblers of the time. "He speaks things, and

you speak words." Berni struck to the core. "*Ei dice cose . . .*" —
"He speaks *things*," and in this Michelangelo is rare not only
among Italian poets. These lines seem to struggle out of the
matrix of language as Michelangelo's "Prisoners" struggle out
of the rock. Seldom mellifluous, frequently imageless (or
making use of conventional conceits), these verses derive their
power rather from a texture of language that seems to be
reproducing the very contours of thought itself: its spurts, its
exaltations, its hesitations, its withdrawals. Sometimes
ungrammatical, these strained hammered lines are undoubt-
edly those of a sculptor. The combination of idealism, sim-
plicity, and crude jest reminds Italian readers of Dante. Again
and again, however, I think of John Donne: there is the same
love of paradox, the same coexistence of contraries, the same
conflict of sensuality and austerity, the same mannered and
overextended conceits, the same war of self against self.

> "*Vorrei voler, Signor, quel ch'io non voglio . . .*"
> "I would want to want, O Lord, what I do not want . . ."

Just as in his sculpture (and in the painted sculpture which is
the vault of the Sistine) *terribilità* coexists with melancholy
resignation, so these poems celebrate all the varieties of love —
of God, of man, of woman, of art, of country — in a similar
grappling of ardor and ashes, the power to do anything frozen
at the brink of a desire to do nothing.

Poems of a man deeply ill at ease with himself and with his
world, the tension is what makes them seem so neurotically
up-to-date. Like a salamander, Michelangelo is always living
in flame; like a phoenix he is always being reborn from the
ashes of his suffering. "A single torment outweighs a thou-
sand pleasures." And indeed there is something masochistic,
passive, feminine in many of the curious images. Like gold or
silver, the poet's desire must be melted by the fires of love,
and then poured into him "per si brevi spazi" ("through such
narrow spaces") to fill his void. But then, as a goldsmith or
silversmith must break the form to extract the work, so he
must be broken and tortured in order to draw forth the per-
fect beauty of his lady. Or, in another poem which is
destroyed by its exaggerations, love enters through the eyes

like a bunch of sour grapes forced into a narrow-necked bottle, and swelling within, is unable to escape. Or else Michelangelo compares himself to a block of stone, which, being smashed, reveals its inner sparks, and then, pulverized, is fire-baked to a longer life:

> So friendly is the inner fire to the cold stone
> that drawn therefrom, contained, it will pulverize
> the rock, embraced in flame, which in another guise
> lives forever, binding others to itself alone.

> And if hardened in the kiln wherein it's thrown,
> It will conquer winter and summer, and be
> more praised than before,
> As purged, the soul will from Hell to Heaven soar
> to dwell with other souls near God's throne.

> So it is with me; If I am undone
> by the fire which plays hidden within me, I must
> be burnt to ashes that I may more life enfold.

> Since if I live, made all of smoke and dust,
> Fire-inured I will endure forever as one
> Not by iron forged but by gold.

The imagery of the first six lines, relating to the preparation of a ground for fresco-painting, is typically masochistic: suffering, being smashed, pulverized, is a necessary condition for the creation and rewards of art. In swift transition, the poet goes on to compare such purgation to the ascension of souls from Purgatory to Heaven and immediately returns to his central metaphor: Suffering enrichens. Suffering is the fiery furnace for the creation of the most precious values.

The initial quatrain of another sonnet expresses with remarkable concision Michelangelo's entire Neoplatonic aesthetic and throws light on his technique of stone-carving as well:

> The best of artists can only select
> the concept which the marble already contains
> within its excess. But there only attains
> the hand that obeys the intellect.

Just as Plato's transcendental Forms or Ideas exist before their specific manifestations on Earth, so the statue, fully formed, exists within the block of marble; there, it awaits the liberating hand of the artist, who finds it by stripping away the excess (*superchio*). Such a liberating hand does not function merely by instinct: it is guided to its goal by intelligence (*la man che ubbidisce all' intelletto*). Thus, the artist is a dis-coverer in the strictest etymological sense of the word.

What is so fascinating is that he is always the same artist whether he is twisting an idea or twisting David's right wrist, whether he is trying to fit the Ancestors of Christ into a spandrel or fit too much concept into too little language. Just as the last great Pietàs and drawings have almost been dematerialized in the effort to render pure Idea, so in many of these poems language is being smashed, distorted, pulverized, almost as if the artist were trying to dispense with it.

I refer only to the greatest poems. Michelangelo, no more than any other genius, did not live only on mountaintops. He indulges in lewd jokes like any Tuscan peasant; he describes the hardships of painting the Sistine "beard to heaven" with the brush over his head "dripping a rich pavement" on his chest; he addresses comic punning lines to the lover of a lady named Mancina, 'Left-Handed"; he lashes out at the bellicose Pope Julius, who was more devoted to the cult of Mars than to the Prince of Peace: "Here helmets and swords are made of chalices, and the blood of Christ is sold by the quart . . ." he writes stupendous sonnets to Night whose dominions may be warred against by a single firefly; and at the last, weary and beaten, he rejects the very arts by which he had always lived, and holds out his hands to Christ, and longs for death to liberate him, as he himself had liberated the perfect forms sleeping within the stone.

All poetry, even the most eccentric and mannered, grows out of a context of existing poetry. The dominant influence here is of course Petrarca, but Michelangelo's molten intensity and convoluted co-existence of contradictions burst the Petrarchian mold even as he seems to fill it. Additionally, and often, one hears the voices of Poliziano, Berni (especially in the comic or bitter *terza-rima capitoli*) and popular carnival versifiers, including Lorenzo the Magnificent. Underlying it all is his beloved Dante: evident less in the borrowing of specific images (although these too exist) than in the tonality of bitter patriotism.

And frequently, even in the most exalted meditations on the varieties of love, the voice is plebeian Florentine: ironical, speaking 'without hair on his tongue', crude-jesting, judgmental. The diction, even the very spelling in the letters and poems, summon up vividly the artist who often preferred the company of stone-cutters in the quarries of Carrara to the humanist theologian-intellectuals at the court of Leo X.

This odd combination of plebeian and patrician, rough and remote, Danteian doom and neo-Platonic transcendence, love of man and love of woman, love of the flesh and repudiation of the flesh is the very power-source of his art, both poetic and visual:

Un sì e no mi muove

"A Yes and No *moves* me! Significantly, the Yes and No take a *singular* verb; they are not two separate (or separable) polarities; they co-exist in a single block and so require a singular verb; the artist cannot extricate himself from the contradiction in which he is embedded.

The astonishing thing about Michelangelo's ceaseless vacillation between ardor and ashes, wanting and not wanting, wanting what he does not want — is that it does not result in sclerosis; he acts in the sense that he makes art out of it. He is goaded, not stricken by turmoil. His works — in stone, paint, language — are the crystallizations of his doubt.

Another paradox. These intense antinomies are often expressed in conventional imagery, for the most part borrowed from Petrarca. The most difficult task of the translator is to convey the magic whereby this happens. For by all logic, it shouldn't happen. Conventional imagery might be expected to convey conventional ideas.

This is what astonished Berni:

Ei dice cose e voi dite parole
He speaks things and you speak words

For Michelangelo's diction, imagery, "parole" — frequently not fresh-minted at all — should simply have spoken "words." Instead they speak "things."

But Berni's praise must not be read as an indifference, on Michelangelo's part, to words. Words are the quarry blocks of poetic art, and when practicing this art—notwithstanding all his too-modest declarations of ineptitude and amateurishness and his submitting of his works to his learned humanist friends that they *riconciarli*: "polish them up"—Michelangelo worked at language with total commitment: revising endlessly, recasting lines, chipping away here, working with the file there, shaping and reshaping toward the ideal shape in his mind. The number of variants proves this; and a study of these variants disclose a true poet at work.

Like many poets then and now, Michelangelo willfully employed ambiguity both as a screen to separate his art from his life, and to intensify the connotative vibrations of the poem.

Hence one scholar might believe a given madrigal is addressed to the "fair cruel lady"; another supposes it is for Vittoria Colonna; a third that it was written for Tommaso Cavalieri; and the sensitive reader, unhampered by scholarship, may read the poem as one listens to music—without denotative imprisonment.

This, I would suggest is how these poems should be read. I have indicated in the Notes those poems which grew out of a specific biographical or historical occasion. But "growing out of" (in the case of poetry, surely) implies "becoming something else"; metamorphosis is not hard evidence. We should be cautious about coming to conclusions about the physical facts of Michelangelo's love-life, or the existence or non-existence of the *Donna bella e crudele* (like Shakespeare's Dark Lady of the Sonnets,) from the poems: delightfully teasing as such speculations might be.

Insofar as true poetry is that state of language which cannot be otherwise, translation of poetry is an oxymoron, a squaring of the circle, impossible. One can only write a new poem, bred on the body of the original.

But in those new poems the dosages of fidelity and felicity range from the word-for-word trot (which is not a poem at all) to the free variation which frequently departs very far from the metrics and imagery and feeling of the original.

Nor can translators of poetry, especially, claim fidelity simply because they are pedisequential, since the footsteps from one language to another do not always follow in the same order.

Add to these intrinsic difficulties of translating verse from one language to another, the leap from one century to another. As I wrote in the Introduction to my translation of Francesco Guicciardini's *History of Italy*: ". . . a true translation, while rendering available to the modern reader the speech of another time and culture, will also preserve the savor of that speech, the flavor of that time. A pinch of antiquity must be added. A good translation of a sixteenth-century text should be redolent of its period. It should bring us back there; we should not only understand it, we should be permeated by it in a kind of historical osmosis, research through the pores . . ."

And later (this surely applies to the poetry of Michelangelo): ". . . to clarify what was ambiguous in the original is not translation but explication. The job of the translator is not to make clear that which was not clear, but to render in another tongue (and sometimes another century) the same degree and kind of ambiguity wherever this occurs."

These were the criteria on which I set about these translations: to be as faithful to the original as possible within the limits of making a genuine poem in English that would re-create the savor and tonality of the sixteenth-century Italian model.

In the sonnets I hewed closely to the Petrarchian rhyme scheme: two quatrains and two tercets. When in some cases such adherence threatened excessive departure from the sense of the text, I altered the stanzaic scheme or used slant-rhymes, or dropped rhymes entirely. The madrigals, which are a freer form to begin with, offered less difficulty, and one could always employ varying line-lengths or rhyme schemes to convey the Italian music. The *terza-rima capitoli* and sestinas are strictly reproduced.

Similarly, on occasion, I have deliberately employed archaicisms in diction for the sake of conveying the flavor of Renaissance speech.

A brief philological note to explain my organization of the poems.

Codicies, autographs, and miscellanies of the original manuscripts of Michelangelo's poetry are to be found in the Vatican Archives in Rome and the Archivio Buonarroti in Florence.

Working from these in his great edition of 1863, Cesare Guasti cleansed the poems of Michelangelo the Younger's bowdlerized publication of 1623, thus presenting for the first time the authentic text. Guasti's organization was by poetic categories: Sonnets, madrigals, sestinas, capitoli, epitaphs, etc.

In 1897, the German art historian Karl Frey put together a new organization of the poems, based on his deductions regarding the chronological order of their composition, and reconstructing under a single group, the sheaf of poems intended for publication in 1546 by Michelangelo and his friend, Luigi del Riccio.

In 1960, Enzo Noè Girardi issued the edition, which has become by now almost canonical, organized strictly according to chronology. Girardi's dating, however, differs from Frey's since he brought to bear a fuller consideration of the sheets of drawings on which many of the autographs of the poems are to be found, the dating of these drawings and speculation whether these relate to the same period as the poem written on the same sheet, as well as a more intensive study of Michelangelo's handwriting, the dating of the paper, etc., etc.

Furthermore, because the intended del Riccio publication had been abandoned and the final selection seems tentative as it has come down to us, Girardi simply broke up the group and redistributed the poems according to what he believes is their chronology.

As I explain in my headnote to the del Riccio Collection on page 141, I have reinstated Frey's reconstruction of the intended publication because I believe that such a selection, tentative though it be, casts light on the poet's critical values and perhaps on some mysteries of his eros as well.

Therefore, I follow Girardi's chronology (with some exceptions) up to 1546 (extracting those poems which were chosen for publication), then present the del Riccio Collection as Frey has reconstructed it, and continue with poems dated after 1546, mostly according to Girardi's datings.

In several cases, I have not been convinced either by Girardi's or Frey's datings; the reasons for my placement of these poems is explained in the Notes.

THE COMPLETE POETRY OF

Michelangelo

Felicity though it last many years
One instant changes to laments and tears,
And those of ancient and illustrious lineage
Are replaced by others in one moment's umbrage.

Whatever moves under the sun death will derange
And conquer quite, and all its fortune change.

[2]

Only I, burning, remain in the shade
When the sun has spent its rays upon the glade;
All others for pleasure, but only I,
Prostrate upon the earth, lamenting, lie.

Grateful and happy, once in my youth,
I could sustain and defeat your hail of harm and ill
But now often against my own will
Weeping I walk, yet I know your worth.

And if your hurtful erstwhile swarm of arrows
Never struck home to the target of my heart,
Now you can avenge yourself, for all the blows
Are mortal that from your fatal eyes depart.

How many springes, how many a snare
Did the little bird elude for how many years?
Only to die a worse death: misfortune's jewel?

And so with me, ladies, whom you see Love did spare
For so many years through tempests and fears
Only to yield me up at this age to a death more cruel.

[4]

How joyous and interlaced with flowers
are those terraced garlands in her golden hair,
vying to be the first to kiss her there
before the others sprinkle down their showers.

And how content all day is that gown
which binds her bosom, then seems to swell and blush;
And that golden net which never ceases to brush
against her cheeks, her throat, her maiden down.

But happier still that ribbon seems to me,
pricked in lamé, tempered so perfectly,
pressing and caressing her breasts like a lover.

And around her waist that girdle, frank and true,
seems to say: Here would I clasp forever —
What then is left for my poor arms to do?

Autograph of a caudal sonnet, that is, a sonnet elongated (with a 'tail') beyond the usual 14 lines. Alongside the verses is a sketch of a nude man painting a fresco above his head, obviously a wry reference to the artist's labors on the Sistine Vault, 1508-12, which would set terminus dates for the sonnet (see #5, over).

Giovanni da Pistoia was a literatus, a functionary in the Medici duchy, and later in 1540, Chancellor of the Florentine Academy. We know of five sonnets by Giovanni addressed to Michelangelo.

[5]

To Giovanni, the one from Pistoia, on Painting the Vault of the Sistine Chapel (1508–12)

I've already grown a goiter from this toil
as water swells the cats in Lombardy
or any other country they might be,
forcing my belly to hang under my chin.
    My beard to heaven, and my memory
I feel above its coffer. My chest a harp.
And ever above my face, the brush dripping,
making a rich pavement out of me.
    My loins have been shoved into my guts,
My arse serves to counterweigh my rump,
Eyelessly I walk in the void.
    Ahead of me my skin lies outstretched,
and to bend, I must knot my shoulders taut,
holding myself like a Syrian bow.
    Therefore, fallacious, strange
the judgment carried in the mind must fly,
for from a twisted gun one shoots awry.
    My dead picture defend
now, Giovanni, and also my honor,
for I'm in no good place, nor I a painter.

[6]

Against the People of Pistoia

I have received, by your courtesy, your Bull
And read it over and over twenty times
Your teeth chew as usefully as your rhymes
Food for a body already fed and full.

As soon as I left you, an idea my mind crossed
that Cain was among your forebears celebrated,
Nor have you from that stock at all degenerated
For when others have good luck, you think you've lost.

Invidious, proud, enemies to heaven, impious,
the kindness of your neighbors causes you annoy,
Only to your own damage are you friendly and take joy

So speaks the Poet about Pistoia—set in Hell—
Keep that in mind; enough. And if you speak well
of Fiorenza, are you joking? Do you think me fool?

                          Precious that jewel
But certainly beyond your appreciation
for limited capacities lack comprehension.

To Pope Julius II

My Lord, if any ancient proverb truthful be,
surely, 'tis this: He who can, will not.
You have lent ear to fables and gossipy rot,
and rewarded one who's your true enemy.

I am your faithful servant, always have been,
and given myself to you as rays to the sun,
But regrets or grief for my time, you have none,
and the more I strain, the less pleased is your mien.

Once I had hoped by your Highness to rise,
and thought: a just weight and a powerful sword
answered need, and were not echo's prize.

But heaven scorns to plant virtue's seed
here in this world, unless it wish we try
to pick fruit out of a tree, barren and dry.

Rome During the Papacy of
Julius II (1503-13)

Here helmets and swords are forged of chalices
and Christ's blood is sold by the quart,
and His cross and thorns are lances and coins
and even Christ's patience is falling short.

But let Him beware of coming to this town
lest His blood spout up to the stars,
for now they're selling His skin here in Rome
and the road to every virtue is blocked with bars.

Since I wished to squander my treasure,
I undertook work at the pleasure
of him in the mantle: Medusa in Maurentania.

Though heaven may honor poverty and mania,
how can we that great renewal attain
if that other life by another banner is slain?

Finis.
Your Michelagnolo in Turkey

[9]

Who leads me forcibly to you?
Alas, alas, alas!
Bound and held, yet free and untrammeled
If you others enchain without a chain,
And without using arms or legs have captured me
Who will come to my defence
Against your countenance
Whose beauty has enraptured me?

How can it be
that I am no more me?
No more master of myself?
O God, O God, O God!
Who has deprived me of myself?
And nearer is to me, and more to me,
                    than I myself?
O God, O God, O God!
How can one pierce my heart
who touches not my skin?
Remains apart
and yet within?
What thing is this, Love, what enterprise
penetrates the heart through the eyes
And seems in such restricted space to grow;
What happens should it overflow?

He who made the whole made every part,
Then from the whole chose the most beautiful
To demonstrate by his divine art
How excellent his works, how beautiful.

How much less doleful would be sudden death
than to die a thousand deaths from hour to hour
Since in exchange for loving her she would devour
      my life and stop my breath!
      Ah, what infinite grief
My heart feels when my mind does recall
that she whom I so love, loves me not at all.
Rather, says she, to inflict more pain on me,
that not even herself she loves, and that
                seems plain to me.
O how then—if herself she does not cherish—
May I hope that she will pity me?
         O dismal destiny!
then it is true that I must perish?

Without you, O my benison,
How will I ever manage to survive?
If departing from my paragon
I cannot seek your aid, hence cannot live?
then all this sobbing, sighing, pain and rage
Which accompanied my hapless heart on its pilgrimage
you-ward, direly doth demonstrate,
O my Lady, my Madonna, my Matchless One,
my death propinquitous and my martyrdom.
      But if it be my fate
that by my absence bereft
my faithful servitude sink into forgetfulness,
    With it will sink to less
my heart which in your keeping I have left
      And being thine
      No longer is mine.

Fame lays all epitaphs to rest
Neither before nor behind them she goes
Since they are dead and their works deceased.

Day and Night hold converse and say:
—We have in our hasty course, led
                    Duke Giuliano to death;
And it is only just that he should take revenge
                    as indeed he does.
And his revenge is this:
that we having slain him,
He, thus dead, takes away the light from us
And with his eyes closed
has locked ours, so that they
                    shine no more upon the earth
What then would he have done with us,
                    while he lived?—

I see myself as yours, yet from afar
I am summoned to draw nigh the heaven whence I derive
So the spicy bait attracts me to your bays
and like a fish, hooked, drawn to where you are
And since one heart, cloven in two, will never thrive
and small signs of life betrays
To you, therefore, both parts have been given
Whence I remain of little worth, as you well know,
And since one soul, between two goals, must ever go
to the most worthy, then if I wish to be,
I must love you ever, ever sing your name,
Since d and flame.

6/19/2002

(708)425-?
NOW!!

26, 2001
idents

nch.

[17]

A comely and inconstant thing
From such a merciful font my miseries are born.

Uncharitable heart, cruel, pitiless,
Clothed in sweetness and full of bitterness,
Time's creature born, your fidelity lasts less
than any blossoms of a mild winter: fugitive flowers.
Time flows and apportions out the hours,
the worst of poisons to speed us on our way
For Time is the scythe and we the hay.

. . .

Fidelity is brief and beauty does not last,
But together seem themselves to consume,
As your sins, of my misfortune glean

. . .

. . .

Always between us the years would intervene.

[19]

A thousand remedies the spirit seeks in vain
since I was deflected from the pristine path,
Fruitlessly one tries to return there again.
Sea and mountain, fire with its sword and wrath
Amidst all these together do I live,

                    and know not whence
I have been deprived of intellect and sense
by one who has stolen away my reason
and permits me not to approach the mountain.

Every virtue nature did instill
in dame or damosel
that I a lesson learn
the very moment my heart doth freeze or burn
Hence this dolor and this Hell
for never was a man
more unhappy than I am
Whatever anguish, complaints, misfortune may select
the greater is the cause the greater the effect
thus, even in delight, happier than I
no one has ever been, no one could ever be.

You have a face sweeter than winy-must,
Shining as if a snail had there passed.
More lovely than a turnip; and teeth white as parsnip,
Enough to tempt the Pope himself to slip.
Eyes color of treacle or swallow-beaks
And hair more white and much more blond than leeks,
Whence I will surely die unless you succor me
For you are all my fate: the luck of me.

Your loveliness leaves others in the lurch
More than any man painted in a church
Your mouth appears to me a purse of leather fine
Full of beans, exactly like mine.
Your eyelashes seem tinted in the pan as they glow,
And twisted are more than a Syrian bow
Sifting, your cheeks turn red and white and all be-crinkled
like corn poppies on cacio cheese be-sprinkled

And when I look upon your tits erect
I seem to see two melons in a sack
Whence I burst into flame like straw or tow
Although I'm worn and broken by the hoe.
Just think: if I still possessed your
                           charming cup so round
I would follow you midst others like a hound,
So that if having it again were possible
Today — now — I'd do something incredible.

Whoever is born arrives at death
Nor doth Time's flight nor the sun
leave anything alive or spare anyone.
Sweetness will dissolve; and breath
And grief disintegrate
And all genius and words abate
And our most ancient forefathers,
                    noble progenitors
All shadows in the sun become,
                smoke in the wind,
                    in that realm you will find
the happy and the sad, like you
So were they men too
And now, as you see, without breath or
                            even strife
they are, earth in the sun, deprived of life
Everything born arrives at death.
Once our eye-sockets swam with pools of light,
Pupils dancing bright
Now they are void, horrid and black
And time has borne us to this bivouac.

What would you with me? What would you do again
with dry wood and an afflicted heart?
Tell me, Love, tell me somewhat something . . .
                                    deign
to let me know into what state
I have fallen, into what merciless maze.

the years have reached the term of my days
like an arrow that has hit the target
                    Hence should I not forget?
Should not the furious fire of itself be
                    tampered down and smothered be?
            And I pardon thee
the erstwhile wounds you inflicted upon me?
Causing my heart to split, blunting your seige.
For Love, as I have proved, holds no more
                            place in me
            I am no one's liege.
And if your blows deployed a new game and strategy
to my eyes would you have my timid soft heart
to want again what once it wanted at the start?
Now that I, weaker than ever before,
scorn you, vanquish you, as you know well,

Do you hope perhaps through some
                        new form of loveliness
                    to paliate my distress
And once again within me dwell?
            Inveigling me once more
into Love's labyrinthian metaphor
and perilous poisonous feast
Where the most wise defend themselves the least;
Yet, shorter the affliction where
                        longest is the age
And this I know: an experienced sage
Whence I will be like ice cast into flames
Which itself destroys, departs, is never set ablaze.

Death alone at this age tames
all, defends us against your cruel arms,
                    your sharp arrows
                    —Showers of such sorrows—
Death which spares no one
of whatever condition, place, time, or fortune.

My soul, daily with death speaking
takes counsel only with itself and of its own
                    self seeking
As new doubts sadden every hour
And the body from day to day
dreams to abandon that bedraggled bower
And set out on its long-imagined journey.
Ah, Love, how you are ready for that journey:
those deeds courageous, audacious, armed, lance affixed!
So that the very thoughts of death
Proper to their time, which the years bequeath,
          You hunt out of me
to extract fronds and flowers from a dead tree.

What more can I do? What should I do?
Under your regime have you not reigned
Over my entire past the entire time?
So that for me alone has remained
Of all my years not a single hour
          O what deceit! What power,
What device can place me once again under your sway?
                    O ungrateful Lord,
Your mouth bespeaks pity, but your heart death, I say
And the resurrected soul, once abhorred,
Would ungrateful be,
foolish, without esteem, dignity,
to return to that which formerly dealt it death.

Everything born on earth has brief duration
From moment to moment mortal loveliness grows less
Whoever loves knows this yet cannot
                    free himself from perturbation.
the cruel vendetta comes with the great sin

Together they come; and he who is least aware within,
More swiftly to his own undoing does he run.
Why do you wish to set me on this path?
So that my ultimate day,

                        my last going down of the sun,
When I have need of goodness and not wrath,
Should be a day of doom and shame and scorn?

[24]

O many years now, a thousand times have you
wounded me to death, not simply conquered me:
                    and so was I diminished
by all your doing, yet my own fault,
                    my own undoing wished.
And now my hair is white do you renew
your senseless promises? How often do
you bind and unbind my sad limbs?
and spur my flanks so that my vision dims?
my breast with tears swims, my soul with rue?

I speak to you, Love; of you I complain
Freed of all your flatteries, why must you again
Take up that cruel bow and shoot in the void?
Like saw or woodworm boring into burnt wood
How shameful to pursue someone like me
Who has lost all motion, all dexterity.

[25]

I made of my eyes the gateway to my poison*
When I felt free passage to arrogant arrows
Nest and vestibule of suave glances and sorrows
I made of my memories that never fade.

Of my heart an anvil I made
A bellows of my breast to manufacture sighs
And so you have ignited me, set me ablaze . . .
                    . . .

* Lest the reader thinks this is a typo for 'prison', the Italian reads: *porta al mie
veneno* (veleno).

When the master holds the servant enchained,
Without hope, in jail, fettered by fate,
Accustomed to that miserable state
Soon all demands for liberty have waned.

Even the tiger and the serpent by habit tamed
And the proud lion born in woodsy arbors
And the apprentice artist wearied by his labors
Doubles his efforts, nor of his sweat's ashamed.

But fire does not unite with such a metaphor
For if the sap of green wood is spent
Fire warms and somewhat nourishes the cold old man

And so much does he return to his green state once more:
All renewed, enflamed, youthful, without lament
Entirely girded by Love, suffused with its élan

                  And if one mocks in raillery
At old age enamored, what shame it brings
to love a divine being — that is a great lie!

For the soul that is not dreaming in its pleasure
Does not sin in loving natural things
Weighing them well, with discretion and measure.

[27]

Just as wood uprooted from its terrestrial place
Loses its ichtor, and thus combustible
is to great heat or the merest spark, vulnerable,
Sapless, dry, easily set ablaze.

Thus my heart, carried off by one who'll never return it,
by fire fed amidst tears welling,
Now that it's out of its own proper dwelling,
Is it not doomed to death whatever ill offend it?

[28]

Flee love, O Lovers, flee that fire
Bitter is the blaze and mortal the travail
For once assaulted, nothing can avail,
Neither force nor reason nor change of place;
Flee while yet my example displays
How the ruthless arm struck, the sharp arrow did assail
Read in me what your grief without fail
Will be: what an impious pitiless game Love plays.
Flee and do not tarry at the first beckoning
Even I thought to reach accord at any time
Now I feel, and you see, that I am burning

Since hour by hour I am obsessed
by the memory of your eyes, and
                              flattered with expectation
And by this not only do I live but I am blessed,
Force and reason and my ancient inclination
Compel me, it seems, by love and by nature
To gaze upon you whatever time is granted me
And if I should altered be,
Living in this state, I would die in that
Nor would I pity find in any form or feature
Where those eyes would not be
                         — where they are not —
O God, so beautiful are they
Who does not live by them is not yet born
Hence we must say
He who comes too late is forlorn
and born thus, he must at once die
For who is not enamored by a comely eye
Cannot live . . .

He who is armed with love conquers
                    whatever fortune,
Whatever fury, misery, whatever power.

[31]

From the eyes of my beloved departs and flies
an ardent ray of such clear light
that it penetrates my heart even through my closed eyes
Whence limping goes Love
So disparate the load it bears
Bestowing on me only light
the while from me it steals shadows and night.

I live sinning, dying to myself I live and have lived,
Already I am not my life but my sin, and from heaven
Whatever good in me comes, my evil from myself is given
by my own unbridled will whereby I am deprived

My liberty a servant, my mortality a god
have become for me. O unhappy state! O forlorn!
To what misery, what existence have I been born! . . .

Even if, besides my own, all other arms
Seem to defend my every precious thing;
Another sword, another lance, another shield
Beyond my own strength are as nothing.
Such are the wretched habits which have removed
Me from that grace which heaven rains down on every place.

Like an old serpent through a narrow place
So may I pass, shedding my old arms
My habitudes reformed, and removed
Will be my soul alive from every human thing
Covering itself with a safer shield
For against death all the world's less than nothing.

Love, already I feel myself reduced to nothing
Sinful nature is in every place
Despoil me of myself, and with your shield
And your Rock and your sweet true arms
Defend me from myself that every other thing
Be as it has not been, and swiftly removed

While my soul from my flesh is not yet removed
Lord, who can change the universe to nothing
Maker, Governor, King of everything
Little to you it matters to occupy in me a place

. . .

. . .

For of every virile man these are the true arms
Without which every man becomes nothing.

[34]

The life of my love is not my heart
the love by which I love thee is without heart or heat
For whatever's mortal is full of error and deceit
Whereas my love from base thoughts dwells apart.

Love, when the soul from God did depart,
Bestowed on thee splendor and light, on me clear eyes
Which cannot fail to see Him in that which dies
in you, to my misfortune, desire's dart,

As heat cannot be severed from the fire
So cannot my esteem from eternal beauty
Whose provenance exalts who most resemblance shows

Since in your eyes you possess all paradise entire
to return thee where first I loved thee
Ardently I take refuge beneath your brows

[35]

The eyelash with its colored shadow wounds not the vision
by its contractions, for the eye suffers no pain
Wherever it turns, whatever extreme it may envision.

The eye below swings without strain
Uncovering but a tiny part of its great ball
Revealing but an arc of its serene terrain

And so covered, less does it rise and fall
Whence shorter are the lids, swift, sidereal
And fewer wrinkles make, when used at all

The white more white, the black funereal
If it could be, the yellow more than leonine
Stepping a passage from one to another fibral.

though touched below and above its confine
the yellow and the black and the white are not surrounded . . .

Beyond here it was, I was seized by love,
Taken as her merchandise, my heart—nay more—my life,
Here her beautiful eyes promised solace from strife
And here those very eyes denied me that cove.

Thence further on was I bound and then unbound,
Here I wept for myself, and with infinite grief
I saw departing hence from this stony fief
He who deprived me of myself, but would not staunch
                         the wound.

[37]

In me death, in you my life I see,
You distinguish and concede and divide the very source
of my existence, brief or long, as you would

Felicitous am I by your courtesy.
Blessed the soul where Time runs no more course
But by you is made to contemplate God.

[38]

How much sweetness is infused through the eyes
into the heart's chamber, where Love sublime
pierces at a single point Death and Time
Midst growing griefs this is the comfort that endures.

Love, that virtue vivacious and wise
Lifts the spirit, our most worthy cure,
and to my troubled query thus replies:

—He who lives his life from me secure
Lives his life as if he were dead—

Love is a concept of beauty instead
Imagined or observed within the heart's distress
Friend of virtue and gentleness.

. . .

The fierce blow, the pungent arrow piercing
Through my heart—there is my medicine,
But that's my lord's prerogative, not mine,
To make life bloom there where harm is blooming.

And if the first blow was mortal, it seemed to bring
With it Love's message which said to me: "Rise
And Love! Blaze with loving! For he who dies,
Soars from earth to heaven on no other wings.

I am he who in your youthful years
Turned your feeble eyes toward that sense of Beauty
Which lifts you from earth to heaven alive."

[40]

When joyous Love lifted me to heaven from this place
By my lady's eyes — nay rather by the sun,
The merest flicker of her smile and all my grief was undone
Cast from my heart and replaced by her face.

And should I long endure in such a state
The soul which groans and laments, alone with me
Having her beside where she is wont to be.

. . .

High-born soul whose limbs and features fair
Mirror within your chaste and mollient members dear
How nature and heaven can draw near
And shape for us beauty beyond compare.

Resplendent spirit in whom one hopes and believes that there
Inwardly, as on your outward face appear,
Love, pity, mercy are—states so rare
Never so intimately bound with beauty were.

Love seizes me, locks me in beauty's prison
Pity and mercy with gentle glances beckoning
Seem to ring my heart with hopes to the horizon.

What usage, what governance, what reckoning
Denies this world? What cruelty? What ultimate negation
That soon or late death spares not so lovely a creation?

Tell me for God's sake, Love, do my eyes find
truly in what I see that beauty I aspire?
Or if the image is within, shaped of my desire
so that I see a face first sculptured in my mind?

You must know, for with her you arrived; and maligned
me, and robbed me of peace, so that I flared in angry fire;
Yet I would not seek a less ardent pyre
nor of a single sigh be deprived — nor be less blind.

"That beauty which you see really comes from her alone,
but passing through mortal eyes to the soul
grows as it ascends to a higher zone.

And there becomes divine, perfect, whole
unto itself, the immortal would all mortal things enfold.
This beauty, and not that, your eyes behold."

[43]

While I, loving, hope for happiness
Reason complains and remonstrates within me
with fit example and true words to be
mindful of my shame: "Avoid distress!

What do you think to gain from the living sun's caress
save death? Nor will you, like the phoenix, rise withal".
But it's no use, for he who wants to fall,
another's vigorous hand does not suffice.

I know my perils. I am aware of Truth and End
And at the same time, another heart I hospice
which slays me the more I do surrender.

Amidst these two deaths dwells my master:
One I do not want; th' other not comprehend,
Suspended thus, both soul and body I do render.

[44]

While I draw my soul near that Beauty whose signs
I'd already discerned, through the eyes she sees a gleam,
The inner image grows, the outer declines
as if abjectly, without esteem.

Thus adapting all its skills and subtlest file
that I break not the thread, love returns and reverts . . .

[45]

Now must my springs and streams be dry. As sears
The summer sun, so do my sighs parch all delights
If I do not refresh them with my tears.

Thus at times our eternal lights:
One hot, the other cold, keep us in balance tempered
So that the world be not consumèd quite.

And so does the heart which is enamored,
Excess ardor would cremate us to the ashy end
Did not the eye douse it with its humor.

Death and dolor that I long for and defend
Grant me a happy future that permits me not to perish.
For he who pleasure takes, does not offend.

Hence my little bark will not vanish
As I would wish to see you beyond that bank
Where the body in its time must depart this parish.

Too much grief would have it that I survive and thank
My stars and live like one who sees others swiftly departing
Eventually his day arrives too, in solemn rank.

Cruel pity and pitiless pardoning
Permit me to live, though you from me are sundered,
Shattering, yet not our faith extinguishing.

Nor has she expunged my memory, or plundered . . .
        . . . .

If my rough hammer shapes human aspects
out of the hard rock, now this one, now that.
It is held and guided by Divine Fiat
lending it motion, moving as He elects.

But that Divinity, which is heaven dwells alive,
by his own doing makes lovely others, Himself even more;
And since no hammer without another hammer
can be made, from that one Life all other lives derive.

And since more power has the mallet-blow
when it falls upon the forge from its highest point
And this one has flown to the very heaven

I unfinished am and all undone and riven
unless the Divine Smith should deign to annoint
me and help me, alone here below.

[47]

When the minister of my abundant sighs
removed herself from this world, from my eyes,
even from herself, Nature was ashamed,
for she it was who first had wanted and deigned
    to bring her here amongst us. Now all are shaken.
But if the Sun of the Sun is spent and taken,
Let not Death, as it has done of others, boast
For now she is alive amongst the Saintly Host.

    Thus Love has conquered iniquitous criminal death
which thought to quench her departed fame forevermore
and assign her soul to a less lovely fate

    But see the contrary — Her poems illuminate
her life more than in life and speak with more breath
And heaven has her whom it did not have before.

[48]

As a flame grows the more it is flailed
by the wind, so every virtue which heaven exalts
More splendid becomes the more offended and assailed.

[49]

Love, your beauty is not a mortal thing;
No face on earth can ever compare
with the image in my heart which commands the very air
With a different flame and flies upon a different wing.

[50]

What will remain of her, Love, after many years
If Time destroys every form of beauty?
Fame. But even Fame will soon flee
And fade entirely despite my tears
More swiftly than I would wish . . . more or less . . .

Alas alas, for I have been betrayed
by fleeting Time and by the frank mirror
which tells the truth to our fixed glance displayed.
So it befalls: he who commits the error
of delaying too much to the end
as I have done (for my time has flown away)
Finds himself, as I do, old in a day.
Nor can I repent, or prepare, or defend
myself with death so nigh.
My own self-enemy am I
Uselessly pouring tears and sighs to my own cost
For there is no harm like time lost.

Alas alas, reiterating so
I review my past, and do not find
in all those days, one day that's truly mine
Fallacious hopes, vain desire, O
the weeping loving longing sighing
(for no mortal affection is new to me)
All have held me thrall, — there is no novelty —
and now surely truth is far away as well
And I perish from my peril
And time is brief yet dwindles evermore
And even could I prolong it I am weary and sore.

So in lassitude I live and know not where truth lies.
Rather I fear to see what time's moving finger
reveals, nor serves it to close my eyes
For Time has modified my bark and hide. Nor can I linger
overmuch. Death and the soul together
put my state to the test: the first and second.
And if I have not wrongly reckoned
(God grant it so)
then my eternal suffering I foresee,
Lord, for truth misunderstood and ill use of my liberty,
And where to rest my hope I do not know.

[52]

Were it permitted to depart this world by suicide
Thinking thus by death to return to heaven,
Who acts upon such faith would be just, even
living and serving hapless misery with pride.

But since man is not like the phoenix
Rising and reborn in the sun's light and heat
Lazy his hand and tardy drags his feet . . .

[53]

He who rides by night must sleep by day
A moment's rest after nocturnal cavalcades
And so after such pain and escapades
To be restored again by my lord, I pray

Grief lasts not where good does not last
But often one is transformed into the other . . .

[54]

I do believe, even were you made of stone
Yet would I love you so faithfully
that swifter than swift, I would make you come to me
And even were you dead, hearing my imploring moan
I would make you speak to me. Were you in paradise
I would drag you down by my plaints and sighs
But being here and alive and of flesh
My hope of loving you and serving you is still fresh.

I cannot otherwise than follow thee
Nor do I regret this enterprise.
You are not fashioned like a tailor's dummy.
that moved from without, moves within, hands and thigh
And if you were not from reason's path deflected
You will one day, I hope, make me content and elected
for kindness cures even the serpent's bite, I do allege,
Like sour grapes which set the teeth on edge.

No power holds against humility
No cruelty prevails against love.
And obdurance by pity's conquered usually
Just as happiness will sadness remove;
And so, loveliness like yours, which the world has never
        seen,
Assumes within, a heart harmonious, akin;
As a sheath which is straight as an honest life
Cannot contain within itself a crooked knife.

And so it cannot be that my devotion
Not be dear to you, at least to some degree
Just keep in mind one does not find that rarest notion,
fidelity in friends, so easily.

                . . .

                . . .

                . . .

                . . .

When a single day goes by without thee
and peace I cannot find anywhere
Then seeing you, your image clings to me
like food after a fast, to my repair

. . .

. . .

As others die to void their guts again
Which then feel comfort more than they felt pain.

Nor passes not a single day between my hands
when I do not see you or feel you with my imagination
Nor is there furnace or oven which withstands
my sighs fanning it to a hotter conflagration
And when I have her somewhat near and acquiescent
I sprinkle sparks like iron incandescent
and much would I say did she but listen
But babbling in such haste, I hardly glisten.

And if it happens that she laughs at me a bit,
Or greets me in the middle of the street
I take fire like gunpowder and spit
balls as from a bombard of the fleet
or other artillery piece, and if she question me
suddenly I lose my voice. Suddenly
my great desire is spent, capitulates
And hope declines as my power abates.

Within myself I feel I know not what great love
that lifts me almost to the very stars
And when sometimes I would that it remove
itself, I have no aperture, no open scars
in my skin large enough to permit it egress
Minor appear my works and much less lovely I confess
For love or strength the saying is but grace and yeast
And he who flies the highest says the least.

So I live thinking of my former life
How it was before I loved thee,
No one ever had esteem for me
Losing time each day until the sun was brinking

Perhaps I thought to sing in rhyme of peace and strife
Or to withdraw from every other gathering
And if my name be praised or damned in every sphere
Let it be known at least that I was here.

You entered through my eyes whence I shed tears
Like a bunch of sour grapes in an ampollo
Passing through the neck and growing where it appears
wider. So your image within me did flow
from without like the ringing of bells
Or like a skin when the fatty marrow swells,
Entering in me by so strait a way
that you shall never exit, I dare say.

As when the wind inflates a leathern ball
The self-same breath blown into the sweetbread's bladder
Opens it from without, and seals its inner wall
So the image of your sweet face does shatter
me as it comes through my eyes into my soul
And opening there, there is locked forever
And like a ball struck at the first bounce, even
so, struck by your eyes, I rise to heaven.

Because it suffices not a lovely woman
to enjoy the homage of one lover alone
Lest her beauty die with her. Hence, though I can
love you, adore you as I have done,
Yet small is my power to praise your merits aright
As a lame man cannot equal even the slowest flight
Nor does the sun cast its benefits on one creature at birth
But for every healthy eye upon this earth.

I cannot imagine how you set my heart ablaze.
Passing there through my ever humid eyes
should have extinguished the flames of your gaze.
All my defences are weak and vain and lies.
If fire ignites water, all else is useless
to save me from the evil which I long to possess
Save fire itself. O strange to proclaim
that the illness of flame is often cured by flame.

[55]

I've bought for you although it costs a mint
A bit of something with a lovely smell
Because I often know a street by its scent
Wherever you may be, wherever I may dwell
Now I feel certain I can surely tell
Though you may hide (I pardon such intent)
For trailing this aroma everywhere you wind
I would track you down even were I blind.

[56]

I live of my dying, and considering it well,
I live happily in my unhappy state
And he who knows not how such anguish is possible
Let him enter the fire with me, and be consumed by fate,

[57]

If I live more by him who burns and cooks and rends me,
The more wood or wind fans the fire,
The more he who kills me, defends me,
And the more do I rejoice the more painful the pyre.

[58]

If immortal desire which corrects and exalts us above
all other thoughts, should bring into the open my distress,
Then pity perhaps would reign even in the house of love
where now he who reigns is pitiless.

But since by law divine, the soul lives many days
While the body dies swiftly indeed,
The senses cannot adequately praise
or values assess they cannot fully read.

Hence, alas, in what manner will be understood
this chaste longing which sets my heart on fire
by those who always see themselves in others?

Thus my lord denies me days dear as brothers
Since he listens to lies and every falsehood.
Yet he who won't believe is the real liar.

[59]

If chaste love, if supernal pity,
If one equal fortune between two lovers,
If bitter fate befalling one becomes the other's
If one spirit governs two hearts' moiety.

If one soul is made eternal in two bodies, two behests,
Both rising to heaven with equal wings,
If Love with a single blow of a golden dart flings,
Discerns and burns the entrails of two breasts.

If loving one the other, himself neither
With one pleasure and one delight, to the same reward
Which both would reach together with a single breath.

If thousands and thousands would not make up one hundredth
of such a knot of love, such faith, such a binding cord
Only contempt could break it, only scorn it dissever.

You know that I know, my lord, that you know
that I come to take joy in you from nearer
And you know that I know that you know like a mirror
my very self. Then why postpone our greeting? Why so slow?

If true now be the hope that you bestow,
If true the great desire conceded, dearer,
Let us break the wall that divides us, for dearer
the cost and double the strength are ills concealed below.

If I love in you, dear my lord, perchance
Only that which you yourself love most, be kind:
That some lone soul may love soul, do not deny.

That for which I yearn, and learn in your sweet countenance
is poorly understood by the human mind.
He who would comprehend it, must first die.

[61]

If I had believed at first glance
that this phoenix-soul in the hot sun
would be reborn in fire, then I, all undone
in my ultimate years would burn all, perchance.

As the swiftest deer, lynx, or leopard wants
but its own good and flees what causes harm,
So toward such acts, and laughter, and honor would I run
Whilst now too swift and late am I, to my mischance.

But why bewail more, since I see
in the eyes of this happy lone angel
My peace and my repose, for my salvation's sake

Perhaps sooner would have been the worst for me
to have seen him, heard him, if now flying as his equal
He emplumes me to follow in his virtue's wake.

[62]

If fire splits the rock and melts iron,
Born of their own hard loins, their own son,
What will flames do, the hottest of Hell
With a dry sheaf of straw inimical?

[63]

In that selfsame time when I adore you too well,
the memory of my unhappy state
returns to me in thought and bewails my fate
"He loves well who burns well, and there I dwell."

Hence, what shield can I raise against them all?

[64]

Perhaps that I learn more compassion
And laugh no more at another's dereliction
Full of its own virtue, without guide or direction
My soul, once so worthy, has fallen.

Nor know I under what other gonfalon
to enlist. Not to conquer but survive this perturbation.
These cries and tumults of the enemy faction
will not slay me unless your help is withdrawn.

O flesh! O blood! O wood!★ O grief extreme★★
For Thee alone my sin was designed.
So was I born, and so my father, seed and sod.

You alone are good, your pity supreme
Succors my state, foretold, iniquitous and blind
So close to death and so far from God.

★ The Cross
★★ of Christ

1.

A new pleasure, worth more than any,
to see the brave goats scrambling up the mountain,
Pasturing now on this height, now on that; now few, now many,
While the goatherd bubbles verses like a fountain
in rustic rhyme, in notes keen and canny
Sings and then is still, then slowly sings again
While his belovèd beneath the oak, heart hard as iron
stays with the pigs, a haughty female lion.

2.

What joy to see from the brow of a hill
their hut made of straw and of earth,
Someone setting the table, someone lighting the grill-
fire outside under the beech, a propitious hearth.
And someone fattening and tickling the pig, playing in its swill,
And someone breaking in the donkey to its first saddle,
                                                    howling with mirth.-
And the old man enjoying all this and speaking little,
Sitting in the sun outside the door like a beetle.

3.

And from without one sees what they possess within,
Peace without gold and without desire for it,
And the days when they plow the hillside with their kin
They count their blessings to each other and peacefully sit
without locks on their doors, without fortunes to win
or misfortunes to fear. The house left open as chance befit
Then having finished their work, chipper and gay,
Stuffed with acorns, they fall asleep on the hay.

4.

Envy has no place here to show,
Pride of its own self is devoured,
Greed they have for some green meadow
Or that type of grass which lovelier has flowered
Their most valued treasure is a plow

And the share is the gem by which they're honored
A pair of baskets is their only pantry
And spades and hoes their golden vases and cutlery.

5.

O blind avariciousness! O corrupted minds and means!
Which misuse all the gifts Nature bestows
Searching for gold, for property, for rich regimes,
Acting as unyielding pride allows.
Sloth, lust instruct you, it seems,
And harm to others, envy seeks to arouse.
Are you not aware in your insatiable fire
that time is brief, necessities few and soon expire?

6.

Those who in ancient times, simpler and clearer,
Satisfied hunger and thirst with acorns and water
Be that an example, a guide, a light, a mirror,
And curb your delights, your feasting and your slaughter
Lend your ear a bit to what I say, nay aver.
He who rules the world so grandly, that mighty Sire
Forever seeks and never finds the peace and poise
Which the peasant with his oxen now enjoys.

7.

With gold and with gems, and with frightened faces, sally
forth the rich, all adorned and preoccupied.
In every wind, every rainfall they find melancholy,
And auguries and signs they read on every side.
But happy poverty fleeing all this folly,
Finds every treasure, nor thinks whence come or how abide?
Safe in the woods, roughly clad in brown
Without the obligations or litigations of the town.

8.

Having and giving, strange and unfamiliar ways
the best and the worst, the pinnacles of art,
To the peasant all these are simple things and ways,
And grass and water and milk are his world apart.
And rude songs and calloused palms fill his days

Instead of tens and hundreds, accounts, usury's mart
Which he sees sprouting everywhere under the moon
So, unconcerned, he yields himself to fortune.

9.

Honor and love and fear and prayer to God
for his pasture, his herd, his labor under divine rule.
With faith, with hope, with desire for the Good
And for the pregnant cow and for the beautiful bull,
Dolorous Doubt, the Perhaps, the goad
of How and Why — all these have no place on this sod
If with simple faith he adores God and sends
Orisons to heaven, one binds, the other bends.

10.

Armed Doubt limps and leaps like the locust,
(So depicted) trembling by its nature in every season,
like the cane in the swamp, crackling and wind-tossed
And from the belt of scarecrow Why, Reason
hangs many keys, none quite right and all quite raucus
And none can open that great gate of Benison
So he must force the lock, and the portal be pried
And go by night and darkness be his guide.

11.

The How and the Perhaps are strictly related,
Both giants of such lofty stature and substance
that soaring to the sun each seems elated
Hence they were blinded for gazing at its brilliance,
And the beauty of cities is freighted and adumbrated
As the colossal proud hulks make their advance
Groping with their hands for the surest place
Amidst rocks and steep contorted ways.

12.

Poor and naked and alone proceeds the Truth
Which among simple folk is like a sacrament
One eye alone he has but that lucent and pure as faith
And his body is of gold and his heart of adamant
And tribulations make him grow, superb and proud of his worth

In a thousand places is he born, though he die in one
    firmament.
From without he is green as an emerald
And to his followers constant, firm, and bold.

   13.
With honest humble eyes cast to the dust,
Dressed in gold and rich embroidery
Falsehood goes warring only against the just
Seeming friend of all and all gentility,
Hypocrite of ice, covered against the sun's thrust.
Always in court, pretending but humility
And his support, his bolster, and his company
Are Fraud and Discord, Lies and Villainy.

   14.
And now, full of woes and toils comes Flattery
Young, adroit, of fine presence and bearing,
Covered in more colors, silks and ribbonry
than flowers the primavernal skies do bring.
With sweet deceit she embroiders amity
And talks only of that which surely pleasing
is to others; tears and laughter within one wish conceals:
Worships with her eyes and with her hands steals.

   15.
In court not only mother of malign machinations
But their wetnurse too, and with her milk
Nourishes, encourages and defends their augmentations
            . . .

1.

A giant there also is, so high in stature
that us down below he cannot see.
And many times planting his feet he will cover
And destroy an entire city.
He aspires toward the sun, and erects a lofty tower
And yet he does not see it though he try
Because his body, strong and robust as steel
Has only one eye — and that's in his heel.

2.

Below on earth he sees the past abide
And his head is firm and to the stars kin
Two days are encompassed in each stride
of his enormous legs and hairy is his skin
And since up there winter and summer are allied
All seasons are equally beautiful to him
And as his forehead is compeer with heaven
So on earth his feet make plane every mountain.

3.

As to us is a speck of sand
So, under his feet, is a mountain range,
Between the thick fur of his legs is a monstrous gland
of diverse shapes, wallowing and strange
Whales would be flies in that colossal land
And the titan is disturbed and laments in rage
Only when the dry winds blow
smoke or soot or straws into that eye below.

4.

A huge old woman, lazy somnolent
Suckles and nurses that hideous horrid figure
And blind, temerarious and arrogant
She comforts him with impudence and sustains his vigor.
When not with him, she is locked in a cavern rent
out of the rocks behind walls, higher and bigger

When he is idle, there in the shadows is she,
Proscribing the people to poverty.

5.

Upon her gravid bosom, pallid and yellow,
She bears only the sign of her master
Fattens on the ills of others, grows gaunt from good and sallow.
Never satiate, at all hours and ever faster,
Stuffing herself, racing to no terminus, shallow
and halterless, hating others and herself as a disaster
Stone for a heart and iron for arms, the motions
of her guts bestir mountains and oceans.

6.

Seven of their children scurry the world's crust
agitating everyone from pole to pole,
Laying snares and making war only against the just
And each of them has a thousand heads, and for them all
the eternal abyss opens and shuts as they thrust
prey into the pit from the universal shoal
And with their members seize upon us bone by bone
As ivy clings to the wall stone to stone.

[67]

Nature foresees well to harmonize
So much cruelty with so much loveliness
that one contrariety temper the other

Thus might your face my sufferings desensitize
Tempering them so much with careless sweetness
that I am freed of them and I am blessèd rather . . .

Cruel star, rather cruel judgment
By whose will and force I am crushed and bound
Nor did any bright star toil for me in heaven
From the day when my sails were unfurled.
Whence I, wandering and vagabonding, went
Like an empty boat battered by all the winds.

Now I am here, alas, and to the blazing winds
I must launch my boat, and without judgment
Flow the high waves where evermore I went
Thus here below is reaped and pressed and bound
That which earlier above the tree unfurled
Whence I deprived myself of the gift of heaven.

Here I am not borne or driven by heaven
But by the potent cruel terrestrial winds
For above me I know not what's been unfurled
Setting them loose, depriving me of my judgment
Thus by others beyond my own nets am I bound
Is it my fault that unknowingly there I went?

Accursed be the day when I went
Under the stars racing above in heaven
Did I not know that the heart is not bound
By the day, nor the soul forced, even in contrary winds
Against the bestowal of our free judgment
Since only by trials are we unfurled.

Hence, if ever grief has from the heart unfurled
Ardent sighs, or if praying I went
Midst burning winds to Him beyond judgment
Merciful to me in that cauldron of winds
Seen, heard, felt am I, nor opposed by heaven
Yet he cannot be forced who himself is bound.

Thus his actions go astray who himself has bound
And by himself no one's released, unfurled

And as a tree grows straight upward to heaven
I pray you, my Lord, if ever thus I went
I may submit like one who feels no winds
My judgment small beneath your mighty judgment.

He who dissolved and chained my own judgment
Whence I sailed into importunous winds
Since you woke me to him, avenge me, O heaven!

     . . .

[69]

If the heart may be seen in the face through the eyes
No other sign of my flame more manifest.
Have I put forth, hence as my request
for recompense, dear my lord, let this suffice.

Perhaps as these chaste fires do arise
and devour me, your spirit with more faith than I assessed
or thought, will pity take and soon, and I be blessed
Since grace abounds for him who well entreats, I surmise.

O were that certain, O then would be adored
that instant when all at once would stop the hours,
Time, the days, the ancient round of the sun milling!

So that I have — and not through my desserts or powers —
My longed-for lord, my sweet-forever lord
Encircled in my arms unworthy and willing.

[70]

When I am driven out and deprived of the fire,
Then am I dead perforce, where another lives and flourishes
For I feed but on flame and what burns, nourishes
Me and where others die there must I live entire.

[71]

I weep, I burn, myself I consume.
Thus my heat is nourished. O sweet fate!
Who is there lives only to await
his own death, as I, fed by grief and gloom?

Ah cruel archer, you well know the hour flies
Our trials to tranquilize, our miseries abate
with your strong hand, our anguish obliterate.
Since he who lives by death never dies.

I know not if it be the longed-for emanation
of its First Maker that the soul feels,
Or if it is the memory of mankind that reveals
Some other beauty enflooding the heart with illumination.

Or if the fame or dream of someone is a manifestation
in the eyes, and in the heart a presence, real,
Leaving of itself I know not what burning seal
that causes me perhaps to weep now of its corruscation.

What I feel and what I seek and who as guide behooves me
I do not know or clearly see or surmise
Where I might find him, though others seem to show me the way.

This, my lord, has happened since I saw you that day:
A bitter sweetness, a Yes and No moves me
Undoubtedly the work of your eyes.

[73]

If the fire were equal to the beauty that glows
in your eyes: twin hearths known, unknown
Nowhere in this world is there so gelid a zone
that it would not burst into flame like incandescent arrows.

But heaven, piteous of our ills and sorrows,
To sooth this bitter mortal life, what it has done
Is deprive us of seeing the beauty which alone
in you is found, in every bone of you and marrow.

Hence fire is not equal to beauty
For it becomes enflamed and enamored
Only of those celestial gifts it comprehends.

Thus it happens, lord, at this age when all ends,
If you think me not enough molten and hammered,
I am kindled small by small capacity.

From sweet sighs to dolorous laughter,
from an eternal to a transitory peace,
have I fallen. Where truth is mute, where never cease
the senses' domination now and after.

Nor do I know if my heart or your face did bestir
this guilt, this grief which the more it doth increase
the less it doth displease; or was it set afire
by the blazing torch of your eyes robbed from Paradise?

Your beauty is not a mortal thing
But made in heaven and brought here, divine,
Whence I losing burning am comforted and strong.

Nor close to you can I be otherwise. In fine
If heaven decrees the arms which my death will bring
Who can, should I die, say you were wrong?

[75]

Felicitous spirit who with ardent zeal and mind
Keeps my old heart alive, dying of infirmities
And midst your thousand other good works and charities
You choose me alone among more noble kind.

As once in my eyes you were, now in my thoughts I find
You come to console me with new sonorities
Whence it seems hope curbs despondencies
Which are, with the soul's desire, close aligned.

Wherefore finding in you, one who speaks for me
And thinks of me amidst so many obligations
He who now writes sends his gratitude.

For it would be but ugly usury and rude
To give you gifts of my disgraceful pictures and creations
In exchange for such a lovely living personality.

I believed the first day I saw and admired
So many forms of beauty, unique, without compare,
That I could fix my eyes like an eagle in the air
Upon the least of the many I desired.

But then I knew by error was I inspired,
For he who seeks without wings to follow an angel there
is flinging seeds upon rocks, and words to winds, and mere
intellect to God. Thus vainly I aspired.

Hence if I approach, my heart cannot support
Such infinite beauty which, dazzling, blinds the eyes,
Nor from afar assures me or trust instill.

What will become of me? What guide or escort
Might ever shield or solace me against surprise
If I draw near, you burn me; if I depart, you kill.

No other figure can I conceive
Either of fantasmal shade or terrestrial body
So that my will might be armed against your beauty
With loftier thoughts that do not deceive.

For stirred by you I seem to fall into such a pit of grief
that Love deprives me of all valor, despoils me
And thinking then to minimize my melancholy
Sends death, duplicating it, to my relief.

However, it's no avail spurring my flight and trial
Doubling my speed against the attractive foe
For the slower cannot the swifter ever surpass.

Love with his own hands dries my eyes, alas,
Assuring me that all this toil is sweet and must be so
For that which costs so dear cannot be vile.

[78]

In your lovely countenance I see, my lord,
What can in this life but poorly be told:
The soul, still vested in its flesh, your very face and mould
has already and often God-ward soared.

And if the vulgar vile malicious horde
Reads itself into the feelings others hold,
No less welcome and intense are desires manifold
of love and faith uncorruptedly adored.

Into that fount of mercy where we all drink
flows every stream of loveliness we see on earth
And they discern it best who are most wise.

No other taste of heaven, no other fruit from the skies,
Thus loving you with faith is a rebirth
in God transcendant, and death is sweet at that brink.

[79]

Just as pen and ink already contain
the high and low and mediocre style,
So within the marble is the image rich or vile
According as our talent draws them forth with our brain

So perhaps within the core of you has lain,
Dear my lord, as well as pride and guile
Also pity in a humble habit, sweet and gentle
Although I've not yet learned to draw it forth again

Animals meadows woods and pebbles
Remedy for our ills contain, and would reveal them unbidden
each of them, if like us they could speak

Perhaps my health and what would cure my troubles
of every ill lies within you hidden . . .

. . .

Francesco Berni, the famous burlesque poet, had sent from Venice to his friend in Rome, the friar-painter Sebastian del Piombo, a *capitolo* in terza-rima in which he sings the praises of their friend in common, Michelangelo:

> I have seen some of his compositions.
> I am ignorant and yet I would say
> I've read them all in the light of Plato.
>
> So that he is a new Apollo and a new Apelles.
> Be still! Enough of pallid violets,
> and liquid crystals and slender beasts.
>
> He speaks things and you speak words . . .

Berni, of course, is constrasting Michelangelo's essential poetry to the swarm of Petrarchian warblers and poetasters in Cinquecento Italy.

Michelangelo's reply in the name of Fra Sebastiano is headed in the manuscript:

Reply of Buonarroto in the Name of Fra Sebastiano

My Lord, once I had heard from you, with proper brio
I went searching amongst all the Cardinals
And greeted three of them on your behalf—Addio—

To the chief physician★—Medico—of our woe
I showed the above, at which he laughed so much, it seemed
His nose split his spectacles in two.

And he whom you serve, so saintly, so esteemed,
Here and there, everywhere, just as you write
Also took pleasure in it and laughed and beamed★★

★ Pope Clement VII (Giulio de' Medici)
★★ Cardinal Ippolito de' Medici,

As for that one who keeps secrets locked tight*
for the minor Medico, I've not seen him yet. Were he a priest
He too would enjoy what you indite.

And there are many others who deny Christ
Because you're not here, and do it without trouble
Since who believe the least are loved the most.

Now with your poem I'll deprive all that rabble of their
lust to see you, and whoever's dissatisfied,
Let him be drowned by the executioner.

the Flesh** cured in salt, drawn and dried,
which still serves well as a charcoal roast
Remembers you better than his own hide.

And our Buonarroto who adores you most
Having seen your verses, if I judge well,
Soared to Heaven a thousand times an hour, like the Host.

And he affirms that the life within his marble
Does not suffice to immortalize your name
As do your divine poems which make him eternal.

For neither summer nor winter can harm them or defame,
Exempt from time and from cruel death,
Beyond whose control rest his virtue and his fame.

And as your (and my) faithful friend sayeth:
"Having seen those beautiful verses, if they hang
Votos before paintings and light candles beneath

them, even I am numbered amongst the throng
Dug out of paint-pots and brushed on plaster slaken
By a clumsy worthless painter. There I belong.

* Cardinal Ippolito's secretary, the Modenese humanist Francesco Maria
  Molza.
**An allusion to the protonotary monsignor Carnesecchi (dry meat) to
  whom Berni had asked fra Sebastiano to send his greetings.

Thank Berni for loving me. At least I'm not forsaken
For among so many he alone knows the truth
that those who praise me are greatly mistaken.

But his discipline might bring me, forsooth,
Serenity and full illumination, and that will be a great miracle
To make a real man out of a painted one that cannot move."

Thus he spoke to me, and I in courtesy withal
Send you the greetings, as well as I know how,
of the bearer of these scribblings and all.

While I am writing verse on verse, redder than red I grow
Thinking to whom I'm sending these gross and clumsy rimes
Since verse-making's not my profession, I surely know

Nonetheless I too send you greetings in these lines
Nor can I think of anything else to say.
I am humbly yours, at all places, at all times.

To you who must be numbered amongst the rare ones of our day
I offer everything and do not think
I will be lacking unless my cowl drops off along the way

Thus I pledge and vow to you; rest assured not a wink
that I do for you would I do for myself
Nor hold me not in disdain that I'm a monk.

Command me. Then just do it yourself.

Terza-Rima on the Death of
Michelangelo's Father, 1534

Although my heart already warned me in anticipation
Believing for my relief the painful pressure
Might issue forth in tears and lamentation.

Fortune at the font of such humor
fattens the roots and swells the veins once more
by death, and not by minor grief or lesser dolor

At your departure, whence it is right and proper
that between your son's first* and your death after
I distinguish. And now I speak of you. With pen and tongue,
    I suffer.

One was my brother, and you our father
For him Love, for you Duty—thus compound
Is my anguish. Nor know I which pain afflicts me more.

Memory paints my brother in my mind
And sculpts you alive in the center of my heart
And more than before, am I pallid with pity. Yet I find

Consolation in the thought that my brother paid his debt
When it was due bitter-green, but you mature.
For those who die old one should not grieve. Or forget

that as one ages, less cruel is nature
Insofar as Necessity
Separates Truth from Sense, and renders it secure.

*A reference to the death of Michelangelo's brother Buonarroto in 1528.

But who is there, despite destiny,
does not beweep his father's death? Coffined he lies
Never more to be seen whom we've seen so frequently.

Our intensest grief, our sorrows and our sighs
Are more or less as each one feels them within hidden,
And Thou alone, O Lord, understand my cries.

And if the soul yield peacefully to reason
held tightly in leash, yet all the more abound
our sufferings after that brief season.

And if the thought to which I have plunged
Were not that those who die well, laugh in heaven
At those who fear death in this world. Thus is expunged

My grief, which otherwise would grow. Thus even
the most dolorous keening's tempered by the belief
that those who lived well, nest even better in Death's haven.

So oppressed is our intellect by that thief
—the Flesh's infirmity—that dying displeases most
those who false persuasions most affirm and believe.

Ninety times has the sun dipped his luminous host
and bathed his shining face in the ocean
before you arrived at divine peace at last.

Now that heaven's taken you from all this misery and commotion
O pity me who still lives, though dead, under this sign
Since it so happens I was born here by your intervention.

Thou are dead to death and made divine
Nor do you fear vicissitudes of life or desires
Not without envy do I write these lines

Nor do you seek to trespass the threshold and shires
of time and fortune which in us inculcate
Doubtful pleasures and certain griefs and fires.

No cloud obscures your light, nor soon nor late
no beclocked hours enchain your effulgence
Chance or necessity are alien to your estate

Your splendor is not bedimmed by night's dark expanse
Nor increased by day, brilliant though it be,
When the sun renews our warmth with its effulgence

By your dying I have learned how to die
O my dear father, and thinking of thee
There where the world rarely permits us to be

Death is not, as some believe, the worst calamity
For one whose final day transcends the first day
Through grace, nigh the Seat Divine eternally

Where by God's grace I presume and assume and say
you are, and hope to see you there, should reason lift
my cold heart out of terrestrial slime and clay

And if between the father and son the highest love and gift
grows in heaven where every virtue grows . . .

[82]

I would want to want, O Lord, what I do not want.
Between the fire and the heart an icy veil is hidden
Which extinguishes the fire whence does not correspond the pen
to the work and makes a lie of the page.

I love Thee with my tongue, and then I grieve that the tide
of that love reaches not my heart, nor know I how
to open the gate to grace that it overflow
and flood the heart and shatter pitiless pride.

Rend that veil, Lord, smash that wall
which by its hardness blocks from us all
the sun of your light, quenched in this world.

Send that light to us, predicted and unfurled,
to your beautiful bride send it, so that I blaze
without doubt in my heart and Thee alone praise.

[83]

Towards others merciful, merciless toward self
is born an ugly worm which by grief is torn
to glove the hands of others skinning itself
And only by death, one might say, becomes well-born

Thus fate would seem to wish that my lord adorn
himself alive with my dead skin
So like a snake in the rocks shedding himself,
Only by death can I change my condition.

O were mine alone that hairy hide
which interwoven with his skin creates the cape
which by luck embraces such a lovely shape!

Let it be mine at least by day. Or the slippers
which base and column of that day provide
that I might bear it yet two more winters.

[84]

Like dry wood in an ardent flame
May I burn if I love you not with all my heart
And let my soul be lost if it seeks another name.

And if by another love apart
from your eyes I am enraptured, by another beauty scalded,
Then let your eyes be removed and with them my life depart!

If I love you not, adore you not, let my audacious
thoughts dissolve with hopes that are hapless
As your love is rooted-firm and you are gracious.

[85]

Wherefore must I give vent to my intense desire
With plaints and sighs and words of melancholy,
If heaven which vests each soul with its own destiny
Does not divest it of that fate late or ever?

Wherefore then does my weary heart still fan my fever
That I languish still, if everyone must die?
And so the final hour less troublesome will be
Since any woe whatever outweighs any good whatever

Therefore if I cannot ward off the blow
which I steal from him and snatch away, if it be fated so
Who will intervene between sorrows and caressing?

If conquered and captured must be my blessing
Then it is not strange that naked, alone, without might,
I remain prisoner of an armed Knight.

Now while Phoebus enkindles the entire hill,
Should I, at such a propitious moment
Soar while I can from earth to firmament
Upon his wings and sweeten death still.

Now is he gone from me. And if vain was the promise
that the flight of happiness would be less precipitous,
the reason is clear: for the soul sinful and ingrate,
Pity will close its hands and heaven its gate.

His feathers were my wings, his hill my stairs
And Phoebus the lantern at my feet. Then without cares,
Death was no less salubrious than marvelous

But dying now alone, my soul is calamitous,
Nor does the memory of such days refresh the heart's desolation
For too late, and after grief, who offers consolation?

Merciless to me certainly
was Heaven when it tempered your living beam
into two eyes alone. So its eternal emanations seem
to grant us the light and you the journey.

O bird felicitous who over us has such advantage
Phoebus is your familiar, and his famous luminous visage
But more than such great seeing, you can as well
Fly to the peak where I was ruined and fell.

[88]

Since Phoebus does not enwind and encircle
this cold and mollient damp globe with his lucent arms
The vulgar choose to rename that sun whose charms
they do not understand, as Night. And so fragile

is it that should one light a tiny torch there
it will deprive Night of its very life. And so tender
is it that a pistol flash rips it asunder
and the merest spark and tinder tears it beyond repair.

And if with all this, she is still something of worth
Daughter of the sun is she, and of the earth
One contains the shadow which the other creates.

But let her be as you will, to praise her is an error —
A widow, dark and so jealous of her estates
that a single firefly can make war on her.

[89]

O night, O sweet time, black though you be,
All striving breaks through to peace at the end
And he who praises you, sees far, and comprehends
And sound is he who honors thee, and thinks judiciously

You cut short and truncate all thoughts wan and weary
Consigning them where dank emollient shadows and silence blend
And from the lowest to the loftiest sphere, you send
me dreaming where I hope to go eventually.

O shadow of dying which puts a terminus
to all that misery which holds heart and soul in odium
And is the last and best cure for our affliction

You render healthy our infirm flesh and infections
You dry our tears and all fatigue allay, and thus
Expel from the just all anger and tedium.

[90]

No mortal thing did I behold
When I found profound peace in your astonishing eyes.
But within, where all evil does displease
I was assailed by a love like to the soul ensouled.

And were it not shaped in God's own image and mold
Only that beauty would it want which the eyes please
But since this is fallacious, only to Ideas
and Forms universal does it transcend and enfold.

I say the living cannot be assuaged by the dying
Nor does it seem you can discern the Eternal in Time flying
Where everyone is ever changing his skin,

Sense is unbridled lust which kills the soul within.
It is not love. Friendships may be perfected by our love
But death does more for them in Heaven above.

[91]

I say to you who to the world chose
To give soul and body and spirit all together
In this dark casket you shall repose.

Regarding this fragment, Michelangelo the Younger wrote: "Bernardo Buon-
talenti said that Michelangelo had drawn, half way up the staircase in his
house in Rome, a skeleton in chiaroscuro, standing with a casket (*cassa*) on his
shoulder, rough, whereon this was written.

[92]

If Lady—though you be
by your beauty a divinity—
Yet you can, like any mortal thing,
eat and sleep and speak here amongst us. If thus
Mercy and grace you bring
And all doubt erase,
In such case
Not to follow you in Love's intent
would be a sin beyond all punishment.
For one with blind eyes
who in his thoughts arrives
at falling in love, though late,
of his own making, no doubt.
O sketch upon me from without
as I do on the candid page and slate
Which having nothing within, imprints what I dictate.

[93]

Now all her charms, caresses, affectations
Now empearled amidst the festival
Who would ever discern the perturbations
the human effort beneath it all?
in the divine bearing of this creature?
whose every feature is made manifold
Whereby silver and gold
reflecting her light, double their own
And every precious stone
More luminous by virtue of her eyes
than of their own intrinsic qualities

The best of artists can only select
the concept which the marble already contains
within its excess. But there only attains
the hand that obeys the intellect.

the evil that I flee, the good I elect
likewise do you, O Lady, proudly retain
hidden within your divine grace. And that I die in pain
my art runs counter to my project.

Blame not therefore for my misfortune
Your beauty or severity or scorn
or my destiny or fate or whatever

Since within your heart you contain together
Death and mercy. But my talent, poor of worth,
knows, for all its longing, to draw forth only death.

Just as by cutting away, O Lady, one extracts
from the hard alpine stone
a living figure which alone
grows the more, the more the stone diminishes.
So all our acts
and all good works for the soul
trembling still for its divine goal
are, in the excess of one's own flesh, hidden
within the crude coarse encrusted skin.
You, however, you alone
can draw forth from me
that which lies in my remotest extremity
I have no other course
for of myself and in myself there is neither will nor force.

If one is bound by a great pleasure bestowed
As if one were returned from death to life
How could one repay such help enough,
Rendering the debtor free, and cancelling what was owed?

And even were that possible, then would be removed
The superimposition of a boundless recompense
to the well-served; whence would be impeded the chance
of grace from that face, contrarily to be approved.

Therefore that I hold aloft your kindness
O Lady, beyond my own possibilities,
I long to be ungrateful rather than courteous;

For when both equally enjoy satiety
Then she whom I love well will no more be my mistress
For Lordliness does not admit of parity.

[97]

What file grinds away
at your weary carcass day by day
—O sick soul!—
And when your mortal spoil
is diminished and decreased
will you be released
of Time, then? And return to where you once were,
in Heaven, in pure
and primal joy, without sin?
Having cast aside the perilous mortal veil?
Yet though I change my skin
in these final brief years
—O it's to no avail—
I cannot change my old, my ancient ways,
the passing of the days,
for all my fears, constrain me and compel me anew
Love, I cannot conceal from you
How much I envy the dead.
Fearful for itself, in me enmeshed
The soul trembles in the bower of my flesh
O Lord, at the final hour
Extend toward me your pitying arms until
You take me from myself and make me what you will.

As a faithful exemplar of my vocation
I was at birth a sense of beauty given
Which is lantern and mirror of both my arts.
If anyone think otherwise, it is false opinion
This alone lifts my eyes to the heights of that vision
Which prepares me to paint or sculpt in these parts.

If rash foolish judgments drag down to sense
even that beauty which stirs and bears to heaven
every sane mind, every right intelligence
Infirm eyes do not rise from the mortal to heaven's portal
Even those fixed steadily upon that high place
For vain is the idea of ascending without grace.

If the comfort of the eyes someone too much constrains
by use, reason also will depart
and lose its way and know fears and pains:
the more deceived
by that which is the more believed,
Whence depicts the heart
as beautiful that which ranks below
even most modest beauty's show
Lady, I assure you,
neither comfort nor use has captured me
So rarely do my eyes behold your eyes
Circumscribed where seldom flies desire.
One instant alone set me afire
Once alone sufficed that I enraptured be.

O not yet healed, Love, even the oldest, even the smallest wounds
You inflicted with your golden arrows
Yet the mind foresees worse sorrows
than those with which the past abounds
If now in old age, such wounds weigh less
I should withstand all evils and distress
Unless you wage war against the dead
But if you feather your bow
to strike me now that I limping go
—naked, ancient, hoary-head—
under your eyes' insignia, assailing hearts,
Killing more than the fiercest darts
Who will comfort me?
What helmet and what shield?
Only flight which honors my defeat
And dishonors thy incandescent assault
O weak old man, it is too late!
Too late to escape and flight too slow
and there where I must go
is there where I must yield
For he who conquers fleeing, remains not in the field.

The following group of fifty poems in memory of Francesco (Cecchino) Bracci (forty-eight epitaphs in quatrains, a madrigal and a sonnet) were written by Michelangelo at the request of the lad's uncle, Luigi del Riccio. Cecchino Bracci, much beloved by his uncle, died at the age of fourteen on the 8th of January 1544. Riccio wanted the artist to provide a sculpture and epitaph for the tomb, and fortified his request with gifts of food and delicacies for Michelangelo. The poetry was written during the course of that same year 1544 and sent individually or in groups to Riccio as they were composed, many of them accompanied by facetious cynical burlesque notes oddly at variance with the funereal compositions.

1.

If here his lovely eyes lie closed under this tombstone
before their time, take comfort yet in this instead:
When they were alive, pity for them was dead
Now they are dead, many live by them alone.

2.

If you have any pity, late or soon,
for me here enclosed, freed of the world's embrace
O save those tears bathing breast and face
for him who remains subject to fortune.

3.

—Why O Death did you not intervene
in faces wracked by the years? but too soon let me die?
—Because agèd things broken by the world do not fly
heavenward and there dwell serene.

4.

Death did not wish not to kill
with its weaponry of years and excessive days,
that Beauty lying here, so that it may rise
to Heaven, its beauty unblemished still.

5.

The beauty which here lies, in this world so surpassed
by far every other lovely creature,
that Death being at enmity with Nature
to win her friendship slew and extinguished it at last.

6.

Here I am, 'of the Bracci,'* feeble in battle
against my death, fighting not to die.
Better would have been 'of the Feet' that I might fly
than 'of the Arms' in defense so futile.

7.

Here am I entombed who but soon before was born,
To whom death came so swiftly so crude
that my soul, stripped of its body, nude
is scarcely aware of the changed state where it's been borne.

8.

He who shuts me here cannot through death
restore to all the others from whom it had been removed
that beauty which on me alive He bestowed and approved,
If at the last he must remake me as I was on earth

> *"Your dead friend speaks and says: If Heaven took
> away all Beauty from all other men to make me alone
> beautiful, as he did, and if, by divine law on the Day of
> Judgment, I must return the same as I was alive, it follows
> that the beauty which He gave me, can no longer be
> returned to those from whom He had taken it, and that I
> must be more beautiful in eternity than the others, and
> they ugly—And this is the contrary of the concept which
> you told me yesterday and the one is a fable and the other
> truth.*
>   *Your*
>   *Michelagnolo Buonarroti"*

9.

The soul from within did not see from without
as we did, the face enclosed in this tomb
But were there not in heaven as fair a dwelling-room
Death could never have removed him thence, without doubt.

* A pun on the name Bracci which in Italian means Arms.

10.

If death over nature is the conquerer
here in this fair face, yet revenge will not fail
Heaven against the earth, by transposing the mortal veil,
divine, more beautiful than ever, from this sepulchre.

11.

Here are closed those astonishing eyes, which, open,
Outblazened those most lucent and holy,
Now since, dead, they shed light on so many,
Whether this be more beautiful than useful, we are not certain.

12.

Here I am believed dead; I who lived instead
for the comfort of the world, and with a thousand souls of
    true friends
in my breast: hence, if only one ends,
one alone from me taken, I am not dead.

> "If you don't want any more of these don't send me
> anything any more."

13.

If the soul remains alive outside its body,
Then mine, which seems to have deprived me of its own being
Manifests itself by the fear I cause the living
Which he cannot do who dies entirely.

14.

If it be true, as it is, that the soul survives
after the body no more lives.
Indeed, by that very dissolution
no longer need it govern
despite itself, and at divine law's behest,
O then the soul, and not before, is blessed
since it is made divine
by death as to death was it born
Hence without sin
Should we laugh away all grief
and proscribed should it be
that for the defunct we mourn

if from the fragile remains,
the dead, beyond misery, true peace attains
At the ultimate hour, the last tick or nod.
So much the higher should be a friend's desire
For it is worth less to cultivate the earth than God.

> *"Not to speak sometimes even if incorrectly in Latin**
> *would be shameful since I'm so closely involved with you.*
>
> *The sonnet by messer Donato seems to me as beautiful*
> *as anything written in our times. But since I have poor*
> *taste I cannot bestow less praise on brand-new clothes, even*
> *those made in the Romagna, than on those silk-and-gold*
> *used garments that would make a tailor's dummy look*
> *good.*
>
> *Write to him and tell him about it and give it to him*
> *with my devotion."*

15.

Scarcely had I seen your beautiful eyes
opened on this fragile life as they were,
when they were closed on the day of ultimate departure,
and opened again to contemplate God in Paradise.

I know and weep, nor was that the error
of my heart too-late aware of their loveliness
But of precious death, rather. Whence to your distress

---

* The Italian text has *in grammatica*, that is, in Latin, referring to the verse: "Hence without sin" which Michelangelo wrote *sine peccata* in the original, instead of *sine peccatis* or *peccato*. His mistake was due either to ignorance or the need for a rhyme: —*ata*.

The note also betrays Michelangelo's self-consciousness about his lack of Latin by contrast with his humanist friends. Messer Donato is Donato Giannotti, one of the leading Florentine exiles, a literary man and political writer, who had written three sonnets on the death of Cecchino Bracci and sent one to Michelangelo.

The correction of Michelangelo's Latin may well have come, with fond indulgence, from Giannotti.

This is the only madrigal in the Bracci collection.

They vanished somewhat for you, but from my
                              ardent desire, entire.*

Hence Luigi, to make the unique form
of Cecchino, of whom I speak, in living stone
eternal, now that he in earth is earth alone.

If lovers each unto the other do transform
since lacking that, art does not ring true
In portraying him, I must portray you.

16.

Here fate decreed I sleep untimely, beyond reach
Nor am I yet dead although I change my dwelling
For I remain alive in you, looking, weeping,
Since lovers are transformed each into each.

> *"I didn't want to send this to you because it's a very
> clumsy thing, but the trout and the truffles would storm
> the heavens.*
> *Remember me always."*

17.

—If two hours have robbed you of one hundred years
Five years are enough to cheat eternity.
—No, for in a single day one lives a century
Who in that day learns everything and disappears.

> *"One who sees Cecchino dead and speaks to him and
> Cecchino replies."*

18.

Great fortune to see myself lying dead
And such was heaven's gift, rather than I grow old

---

* The second quartina of the sonnet in its original version was different.
  Michelangelo sent del Riccio a variant with the following note:

  Messer Luigi. The four last lines of the octave above of the sonnet I
  sent you yesterday are contradictory. Therefore, I beg you to send
  them back to me or insert these instead, so that they might be less
  awkward. Or you fix it up for me.

  This is the only sonnet in the Bracci collection.

Since there was nothing better to give me in the world
Anything other than death was worse instead.

> *"Now I've finished my promise of fifteen versicles of
> credit; I'm no longer under obligation* to you, if nothing
> else comes down from Paradise where he is."*

19.

Earth my flesh and here my bones, devoid now
of their lovely eyes and this charming face
attest to him whose joy I was, and grace
in what prison the spirit lives below.

> *"Take these two verses below which are a moral thing. I
> send you this for the balance of the fifteen versicles:*
>
> *Show him for whom in bed I was so gracious,
> What he was embracing and where my soul lives now."*

20.

If the weeping of others that I might live a second round
Should be as flesh and blood to these bones of mine,
then pitiless were he who in pity pines
to bind again the soul now in heaven unbound.

> *"For the salted mushrooms, since you don't want any-
> thing else."*

21.

He who weeps for me, dead here, hopes in vain
Bathing the bone and in my sepulchre that I might be
resuscitate entire like fruit to a dry tree.
But a dead man does not surge into Spring again.

> *"This clumsy verse, spoken a hundred times, for the
> fennel."*

---

* We can hear the Tuscan voice in the spelling: *obrigato*. Michelangelo like
Tuscan peasants today not infrequently interchanged l's and r's.
   What I have rendered 'versicles of credit' is *pollizini* in the original:
pollizini are pawn-tickets, here used mockingly to refer to the quatrains
Michelangelo was writing.

22.

You alone O tombstone that shuts me in
know if I was once alive; and if anyone remembers,
He seems to be dreaming. So swiftly death dismembers;
that what had been, seeming never to have been.

23.

Beyond the years and hours that enclosed me in this guise
Returning to life, if such could be, from here
More than its departure do I fear,
For then I was born where dying dies.

> "Thus speak the trout, not I; however if these verses
> don't please you, don't marinate them any more without
> pepper."

24.

I was a Bracci, and if Death my soul deprive,
my portrait yet remains; thus Death is dear to me
Since such a work has so benign a destiny
to enter painted where I could not alive.*

25.

Bracci was I born, and after the first wail,
Upon the sun but a short while looked my eyes
Here they are forever, nor would I otherwise
Since I remain alive in him who loved me without fail.

26.

I was no more than alive; dead, I am alive
and dear to those from whom by death I have been taken,
If now he loves me more, much more than a mere token,
Who grows by diminishing, of that death does he thrive.

27.

If death here possesses the finest flower
of virtue and beauty in the world, scarcely open,
buried rather before its time, I am certain

---

* Cecchino's father was one of the Florentine exiles

there'll be no mourning for the old who die at the latest
hour.

28.
My divine and perfect beauty from heaven did descend
and from my father my mortal body only.
If what God gave to me dies with me
What can my mortal part alone from Death portend?

> *"I am returning the melons with this scribble, but the
> sketch not yet. At any rate, I will do it as soon as I'm
> more in the mood to draw. Remember me to Baccio and
> tell him that if I had one of those tasty stews he used to
> make for me up there, I'd be another Graziano today; and
> thank him on my part."* ★

29.
Forever to death but for an hour alone
was I first given to you, and such happiness
did my beauty bring, and then such distress
that better were it never to have been born.

> *"For the turtle; as for the fish Urbino* ★★ *will take care
> of them; he's already gobbled them up."*

30.
Spent here is the sun from which you still burn, still cry,
Its soulful light was a brief adventure,
Less grace and bounty would have lasted longer.
For the unendowed death comes late and lazily.

> *"Fix it up as you like."*

31.
Here must I rest and sleep but for a while
to render beautiful my terrestrial veil

★ del Riccio had sent Michelangelo the melons and a bottle of Trebbiano
  wine, (Michelangelo's favorite) together with a design for Cecchino's tomb
  which Michelangelo didn't like and promised to replace.
★★ Urbino was the artist's faithful and much loved servant.

For more grace and beauty even in heaven fail
to serve nature as exemplar, norm, and style.

32.

If his life and peace were my open eyes,
Now they are closed, who is his life and peace?
Not beauty, no; gone from the world with my decease,
But death alone since all his love here lies.

33.

If alive in the world, I was his very life and limb
For whom now only earth is my beauty,
then not death alone is it, but cruel jealousy
that someone did not die for me before him.

> *"Clumsy thing! the well is dry; one must wait till it*
> *rains; and you're in too much of a hurry."*

34.

Since in wounding others no one was peer
to fair-faced Braccio, here entombed and taken
by Death, as he was, if I am not mistaken
that the less fair be left for him to spear.

35.

Buried here is Braccio, with whose face
God wished to correct nature.
But since the good is lost if not cared for
He revealed him to the world and withdrew him apace.

36.

Here, dead, Cecchino Bracci lies;
His splendor was your life till his decease
Who did not see him did not lose him, and lives in peace.
Who saw him loses his life unless he dies.

> *"The tomb speaks to whoever reads these verses. Clumsy*
> *things! but since you want me to write a thousand lines,*
> *inevitably they must turn out to be of every quality."*

37.

Earth to earth and soul to heaven. Without fail
by death rendered. To those who love me,
In custody he gave my beauty and my fame
to eternalize in stone my terrestrial veil.

38.

ABOVE THE TOMB

Here entombed is Braccio, his loveliness here laid
And as the soul to the body is form inspired
So to me is the work sublime and admired,
for such a sheathe suggests an exquisite blade.

39.

Should it happen, as with the phoenix in the fire,
that Bracci's fair face return even more
fair, it would be well that what we knew before,
We lose for a while and then again acquire.

40.

Extinguished forever is nature's sun
Here with the sun of Braccio interred.
Death killed him without iron or sword
As by a whisper-wind a winter-flower's undone

"For the fig-bread."

41.

BELOW THE HEAD WHICH SPEAKS

I was de' Bracci; here my life is death, among the immortals
Since today the earth was divided from the skies
And I alone in the world soared to paradise,
whereby it clanged forever shut its portals

*"See you again next Saint Martin's day, if it doesn't
rain."*

42.

Herein the noble clay of Cecchin lies,
by death deposed, beneath the sun unparalleled, beyond all
    epigraphs,

Rome weeps for him, and heaven takes pride, and laughs,
Unshackled of mortality the joyful spirit flies.

43.

Here Braccio lies; one could desire no less
a sepulchre for his corpse, and for his soul this sacred office.
If dead, more than alive, he inhabits a worthy hospice
in earth as in heaven, then death is sweet to him and
    pious,

44.

Here death reached out an Arm and the bitter fruit reaps
Rather, the flower; at fifteen years he fell;
Only this stone enjoys him, possesses him well
And all the rest of the world only weeps.

45.

Mortal, I was Cecchin, now divine I thrive,
Little of the world I savored, but heaven's eternity I range
So I am fond of death for such a fair exchange
that gave birth to many dead, to me, alive.

> "Since tonight's poetry was in the doldrums I
> send you four crusty doughnuts for the three
> honey-cakes of the constipated miser. And my best
> wishes to you."
>   Your Michelagnolo at the Slaughterhouse of
> the*

46.

Death here closed the eyes, and body and soul untied
of Cecchin Bracci, premature his departure

* Michelangelo's studio was near the Trajan Column on a street named Macel
  de' Corvi (Slaughterhouse of the Crows) and on the manuscript, instead of
  the word, he had drawn a crow.
      Berlingozzi and berriquocoli are Tuscanisms for certain doughnuts and
  honeycakes, obviously used here as metaphors for the epitaphs. The cacas-
  techi (the constipated miser) might refer to the del Riccio or Giannotti who
  contributed fewer epitaphs.

was, that he might change his life, and secure
What often to old age is denied.

47.

I was de' Bracci. Of my soul death did me deprive
and all my beauty turned to earth and bone.
I beg not be opened the enclosing stone
that fair I remain to him who loved me alive.

48.

That the soul lives, I, dead, am certain;
and certain too that living I was dead,
I was de' Bracci and if time cut me short instead
Who lives less has more hope of pardon.

49.

Celestial Braccio has reclaimed his face terrestrial.
No longer is it here. Before the Day of Judgment it's been carried
from the earth by Pity. If then it were buried,
He, alone, of heaven would be worthy withal.

50.

If heaven lends the soul and the world the body
for a long time, How will Braccio here dead
ever be satisfied? With what goods supplied instead?
Remaining creditor of so many years and such beauty?

"For the fun of it and not for the quality."

If it come not from you, nothing renders
of my eyes a mirror
Wherein the weary heart surrenders,
So that if other beauty I behold
resembling not yours, O Lady, it is dead
as a glass without silvering or lead
does not reflect well, or take the mold
of the outward object.
     So, fit example
   and marvel will it be
    for one who despairs of winning your grace
If your lovely eyes and brows would efface
    my unhappiness
     with true gentleness
   And turn to make me
   Born to misery
So late in life, once again blessed.
If thus by your favor
   grace and good fortune prevail
   Nor harsh destiny avail,
You will have conquered then Heaven and Nature.

[103]

A man in a woman, a god rather
speaks through her mouth to me
Whence I, listening, am made other
than myself, nevermore myself to be.
Yet I am sure,
Since I was taken
from myself by her, my own self shaken
out of myself, to show more pity for myself.
Thus her lovely face
Spurs me beyond dismal desire
For I discern death in all other forms of beauty
O Lady! O my Lady!
By water and by fire
May my soul pass to blessèd days
O see to it then, no matter how I yearn,
that to myself I nevermore return.

If the divine part of us has well conceived
the face and gestures of someone, then with double
strength, from a swift rough model,
he gives life to the stone—that's not by art achieved.

Nor is it otherwise with rougher papers as well,
Before a ready hand takes up the brush
Even geniuses most skilled do not rush,
But test and review, and compose their material.

So it is with me: a model of small price
was my birth, and then I was reborn
into a fine perfect thing, from a lofty worthy Lady.

If my limits are expanded by your mercy
And my excesses filed, what penance will atone
My fierce ardor when you correct and chastise?

[105]

How delightful to a taste balanced and sure
are works of the prime art which assembles
face and gesture, and with members more alive, dissembles
out of wax or clay or stone, a human figure.

If then injurious time, villainous bitter time efface
it, smash it, distort or entirely has dismembered
it, the beauty that once it had is remembered
And vain appreciation transferred to a better place.

[106]

Not unworthy is the soul which attends
eternal life, peace and tranquility,
enrich it with the only money
heaven mints, and which nature spends.

Every time my idol appears
before the eyes of my feeble fierce heart, it seems
between one and the other death intervenes
Hunting all the more, the greater are my fears.

Yet such outrage soothes my soul with content
more hopeful than the joy of any other destiny,
Invincible Love, with its brightest company
takes up in its defense these arms and argument:

One dies but once, it says, and only once is born
And he who dies of my love, what then will be
if even dying, with me he still sojourn?

Love aflame then sets the soul free
And if it be a magnet to ardor similar,
then like gold purged in fire, to God will it soar.

If grief, as someone says, makes us beautiful
then to deprive me, weeping for a lovely human face,
is for my own good, and to be ill is well
and my misfortune brings me life and grace.
For bitter-sweet against my soul,
is that which my vain thoughts desire,
Nor can evil fortune conspire
against one who flies low,
and gyrating, crow
in triumph from a lofty ruin.
Pious and benign,
Poverty nude in solitude
is for me a new whip,
            a sweet discipline.
O more salubrious to the pilgrim soul
            in its duress
either at play or war
is knowing how to lose much more
rather than winning less and less.

—If the face of which I speak, that of my Lady,
had not denied me those glances that beguile,
Love, what further trial
would you have set for me? What flame more fiery?
If seeing her but seldom, it is the same
You burn me yet with her fair eyes and not a little.
—the least part of the game
has he who loses neither jot nor tittle
If in pleasure all desire is delirious
                then, O serious
                in satiety
no hope will there be
nor green again will it blossom
in that sweetness which swallows all martyrdom—
Rather of her, my Lady, would I speak
If, in her abundance she is weak
And yields to that for which I aspire
then your grace could not appease my high desire.

[110*]

Amidst the sweetness of a boundless courtesy
Some offense against my honor and my life lies there
often hidden and disguised, and weighs so heavily
that it renders my recovered health less dear.

To affix wings upon another's shoulders, till it appear
all the while a snare has been set secretly —
O this will quench love's ardent charity
When most one wants it to blaze and flare.

Hence, O my Luigi, keep clearly in mind and understood:
Your erstwhile kindness to which I owe my life and was reborn,
Let it not be by whirlwind rent or tempest torn.

Scorn teaches us to conquer gratitude
And though I'm well aware true friends avoid dissent,
A thousand joys are not worth a single torment.

* See notes 110 and 110A.

[110A]

Though sweet it may be,
too harmful is the gift
wont to bind the soul.
Whence my freedom grieves and laments the rift
Created by your undue courtesy
For your kindness takes its toll:
deprives me of my liberty
More than any robbery.

And as the eye force-fixed upon the sun
is weakened in that very faculty
which is its reason alone for being
Since it is made for seeing.

So my desire does not wish
to hobble my gratitude which grows of your largesse
for my too-little is abject toward your too-much
nor can the former pardon the latter.
                              Only by such
parity in fortune and ability
does love ordain friendship can fare
Hence it is rare.

[III]

Why so late? Why do I not more frequently believe
with firm faith that the internal fire
will blaze and raise me from earth and bear my heart higher
to heights it could not of its own virtue achieve?

Perhaps such intervals are needed for they leave
between one and the other messages of love, a promissory gyre,
For things rare, more force and value acquire
When most-desired and least-near interweave.

Night is the interval and day the light
One freezes my heart, the other it enflames
with love, faith, and celestial fire . . .

Not always a bitter mortal error
is wild passion for boundless beauty
if this melts the heart which then can be
penetrated swiftly by a divine arrow.

Love awakens then with wings feathered
for the higher flight not denied even vain furor
But is a first step rather; thus to its creator
Soars the soul, on earth insatiate and tethered.

The love of which I speak aspires to higher worth
O Lady, and is too dissimilar; a poor recompense
is such ardor in a heart wise and virile.

One draws to Heaven, the other to earth
One dwells in the soul, the other in sense
And draws its bow at things base and vile.

The del Riccio Collection

The following madrigal for the '*Donna altera bella* e *crudelé*—'the haughty beautiful and cruel Lady'—initiates the series gathered together for publication in 1546 by Michelangelo and his friend, Luigi del Riccio, one of the Florentine exiles in Rome.

The selection of course was derived from all the poems the seventy-one year old artist had written up to that time.

Given the tentative nature of the selection (the Casa Buonarroti manuscript contains many corrections in Michelangelo's hand) and the fact that the plans for publication were dropped (because of del Riccio's death in 1546, or a quarrel between the friends), Girardi has broken up the collection and distributed these poems according to chronological criteria.

I feel, however, that keeping the group together (as Frey has derived it from the various manuscripts) casts light on Michelangelo's own judgment on his poetic accomplishments, and this more than offsets the tentative nature of the del Riccio collection.

I do not number the poems in the collection separately, however, precisely because of this tentative nature of the intended publication. In this book, poems 113 to 210 represent the del Riccio collection according to Frey.

[113]

My refuge and my ultimate escape
What more secure and yet less efficacious
than all this weeping and praying?
Which help me not, for
Love and cruelty here pitched in me their tents of war
One with pity armed, the other, death
this one slays, the other keeps me alive
thus I survive
with an impeded soul
denied its own dying
hindered of its own surcease
which alone would bring it peace
O how often has it stirred
to depart for that domain where hope resides
But then
her true image by which I live
flares in my heart again
so that death shall not vanquish love.

Never can it be that her blessèd eyes
should take of mine, as I of hers, delight
Requiting her sweet laughter, her gaze divinely-bright
with my sour lamentations
O fallacious expectations
of lovers!
How can it be
that she
is so oddly diverse, dissimilar?
Her infinite beauty, her luminosity
So far removed from my flame,
my habits, my yearning
that though she share my burning,
She does not burn the same,
Between natures so diverse, so contrary,
Limping Love takes umbrage and from one must depart.
Nor can she fail but pity me
when, into a gentle heart of gentle birth,
enters fire, it seemeth, water issues forth.

Fortress most impregnable your eyes conquer
as they outscale, make pale whatever other splendor,
And if it be that one may die of pleasure,
Now would be the time
                    —a death sublime—
When great compassion commands great beauty.
And if my soul
were not accustomed to the fire
I would be dead already, burnt entire
at the merest promise of your first glances
and so I pay the toll
of my greedy eyes, my own enemies,
Avidly, I look; the lances
strike; nor is it too late, without reprieve
Nor can I grieve
that you cannot do
what is not yours to do
In perfect balance, beauty and compassion will
—the more they offer solace—surely kill
And he who on them looks or turns his mind
Fatally—O fatally!—is stricken blind.

I can no more be silent, Love, nor do I wish to be
although swept in the crescendo
of your frenzy I must speak up, I vow
the more harsh you are, the more bitter to me,
to that much more virtue is my soul spurred
and I am counselled to courage and all my fears deterred
And if at times you seem to express
Compassion for my death, my anguish, my distress
As for one who is dying.
Within me then I feel my heart failing
Lacking its familiar suffering
O eyes of lucent holiness
the modicum of grace I do possess
Is sweet and dear to me. For therein one discerns
that he acquires much who losing, learns.

If it be true that pure desire
bears upon its wing
every lovely thing
from this world to God; thus we aspire,
O my Lady, you alone lift to the sublime
One who has eyes like mine
And thus I neglect
all else, and her I select
Caring but for that
Nor need it be wondered at
that I love her, long for her,
Call her name at every hour
Nor should I be praised
if my soul is by its very nature raised
Leaning upon similitudes
My eyes in her eyes, whence the spirit broods
                              as it descends
And rests in me and defines my ends.

If first love is conceived as ultimate love
                    residing in a realm above
then this honors her by whom one has soared
For one must love the servant who adores the Lord.

Although my heart too often has been burnt by love
And I consumed by too many years
These latent torments and fears
will (without my dying) mortal prove.
Whence my soul desires,
while I am yet encurtained in these fires,
the ultimate day of all my days
will be the first in a more tranquil realm.
No other refuge, other ways
Lend my life respite from doom.
Only by cruel and bitter death
                    can I escape dying
And only death can contravene death
Since any other help is double death
for one who but by dying resumes living.

You alone I behold, content with my ill-content
Yet nothing do I request but leave to love you
Nor can you savor peace without my grief blent,
Nor would my very death suffice to move you
              Nor my demise
                  be the worst thing in your eyes
So am I sorrow-laden
and my heart heaped to the level of your scorn
              So was I born
                to dolor and denied death
For this maiden
Pitilessly will not help me flee this life
But rather wields the knife
and kills me, yet would not that I die
For death is swift, a moment's agony
Compared with your long-drawn savage cruelty
But he who suffers torments wrongfully
Hopes no less for justice
than for pity's poultice
thus the soul, sincere, supports and serves
as much as possible, as it deserves
And hopes not for that which you can do
For martyrdom's reward is not here below.

From near or far my eyes joyfully behold
Wherever your lovely face may appear,
But that power is denied my feet which hear
My arms, my hands, all this mortal mold.

The soul, the mind whole and healthy,
                          are by the eyes impelled
to ascend more freely from this lower
realm to the heights of your beauty. But much ardor
bestows no such privilege on the body, young or old.

Gravid, mortal; so that it must follow
in vain an angel's flight, and wingless fly
And take delight in you simply in seeing.

But if in heaven you a great gift may bestow,
Make of all my body a single eye
So that no part of me but joys in your being.

From the first cry to the final sigh
That brink whereon I already quiver
Who else but I has been allotted ever
So cruel a destiny from afar,
From so splendid, so savage a star?
I do not say iniquitous or rank
Yet better were she frank
and openly disdaining me, truncate this love
          and me remove
          from this maze
But rather she, the more I on her gaze
the more she promises my martyrdom
Sweet pity from her pitiless heart:
          thus am I torn apart
          and stricken dumb.
O ardor so-desired
Only the vilest man makes way with thee
Whence I, were I not blind,
would render thanks for the first and final hour
that I saw her; and error
conquered me and remains forever in my mind,
If lost in her net
one loses only strength virtue and wit.

Everything I see counsels and constrains me
to love and follow you
For where you are not is not felicity
and revel turns to rue.
For love which all other marvels scorns
would have me quest and yearn for my salvation
in you alone, my sun*, my all
holding my soul in thrall
beyond all expectation
beyond all bourns,
depriving me of any higher hope or aim
But would rather that I live in flame
Not for you alone but whoso you resembles:
your selfsame eyes, your selfsame brows,
                              should I be riven
of your presence I am deprived of sight
My eyes, my life drained of all their light
For heaven where you are not is no more heaven.

* The Italian plays with the similarity: voi, *sole*, *solo* . . .

Now it is surely time
to withdraw from this martyrdom
For age and desire chime
not well together. But the soul—you know it well,
O Love—is blind, deaf, dumb
to time and death, so that I still,
in the very face of death, remember her
And if your bow and string
Should split and sunder as the arrow flies
to sting me, dismember me
        yet do I beg thee
that you deprive me not of a single torment,
          nor sufferings nor cries
For he who is never cured never dies.

As you cannot fail but to be beautiful
So you cannot fail but be benevolent
And since you are all mine, malevolent
must be the end of it: you will destroy me, undo me all.

Thus so long as endures
compassion equal to your loveliness
the end of your fair face assures
at the very moment and no less
the end of my ardent heart
But since the liberated soul must depart
        and return toward
its star who is its Lord
there to reap eternally its true reward
where all the bodies of the dead forever dwell
in quietude or grief, Paradise or Hell,
I pray that ugly though I be
here on earth with you, that you would wish for me
even in Paradise to share a place
For surely, a gentle heart matches a sweet face.

If fire is fatal to everything
and burns me too, yet does not cook me entire,
It's not that I am strong, or strength is lacking to the fire
that I find salvation in my suffering
    And like a salamander flourish
    Where others perish.
Nor know I who had deflected me
from peace to such martyrdom elected me
    Surely not your face alone
    Surely not my heart alone
And surely this tangle of my love
Cannot be untied save by the Lord above
Who has placed my very life in your eyes
If I love thee beyond your surmise nor to thy harm
then forgive me as I forgive Love's destructive charm
Which, unlike her who truly is killing me,
Wants me to die, though she not willing be.

How much the more does it seem
I suffer from my major ill
if the waning of my will
is painted on my face, you gleam
the more, the more I gloom
thus my misery instead
but adds to your loveliness.
        And so my dread
becomes delight, and losing I gain,
And she who torments me, does me well
    If your beauty of my pain
      is fed, and your contentment of my ill
O my savage wild star!
What if I should perish?
Would not your beauty diminish?
Since its augmentation is my diminution
And its roots within me are?
If this be true:
    Your sweetness my bitterness
    Your revels my rue
And these be lacking with my death
then dying, I, so would your beauty die
My dolor no longer lending it breath
Then since of my misery is your beauty blent,
    My soul is more content
    and does not languish
For great joy makes bearable great anguish.

So swift, so audacious is my Lady
that when she has slain me quite, her eyes
promise whatever happiness one might surmise
the while deep within the wound
She prods and keeps the cruel sword in me
    Thus do abound
    Death and Life
in all their contrarieties
Tinily together, at strife
within my soul . . . but grace displaces grief
Hunts it forth from me for further trial
For more harmful is the evil of her guile
than the momentary balm of her smile.

On Michelangelo's allegorical figure
of Night in the Medici Tombs
    By Giovanni di Carlo Strozzi

Night which here you see sleeping so sweetly alone
Was by an Angel carved out of the stone.
And since she sleeps, she is alive as we.
You don't believe?—Wake her, she'll speak to thee.

    Michelangelo's response
    (in the guise of Night)

Dear to me is sleep and better to be stone
So long as shame and sorrow is our portion.
Not to see, not to feel is my great fortune;
Hence, do not wake me; hush, leave me alone.

A cold face sets me flaming from afar
Itself frozen, emblazing me to commotion,
Two elegant arms which can move without motion
all other substances, like the radiance of a star.

Unique spirit! I alone comprehend who you are:
Deathless, yet death-dealing to others is your potion,
Unbound, yet binding my heart; without emotion
dispensing only joys in me that griefs bestir.

How can it be, my lord, that your calm countenance
Should cause in me such contrary effects intermitted?
If poorly can one bestow what's not there to behold?

Whence, if you've deprived me of a happy life, perchance
You're acting as if the sun, were it permitted,
Were to warm the world, and be itself cold.

With your eyes I see sweet shimmerings
Which my blind eyes can never contemplate,
On your limbs I bear the heaviest weight
Whereas my limbs are weak and stumbling things.

Featherless I fly on your wings,
On your genius moved evermore to heaven
Your judgment makes me pale or blush even
Freezing in the sun, hot when cold fog clings.

In your desire alone is my desire
My thoughts are forged in your heart
My words take breath with your breath.

So alone it seems I am the moon whose fire
is borrowed, for our eyes can only see that part
of heaven the sun illuminates beneath.

Every covered place, every closed room
Whatever is by nature circumscribed
Contains Night even while daylight thrives
Playing its luminous game against the sun

And if by fire and flame it's vanquished and undone
And if by sun hunted and of its divinity deprived
Even to the vilest thing may that be ascribed:
Any glowworm may shatter it late or soon.

Whatever lies open to the sun
Warms a thousand seeds a thousand plants to display,
the proud plowman plows to the root.

But in shadow alone is man planted and begun,
Hence Night is more holy than the day
As man is worth more than any other fruit.

He who out of nothing created Time
that did not exist before for anyone
dividing it, gave one part to the sun,
the other to the moon, closer, if less sublime.

Hence chance, fate, fortune He did assign
In one nascent moment for everyone
And I was assigned the hours dismal and dun
like me at birth and in my cradle—the same sign.

And like one who transforms himself,
When it is deepest night to darkest night
So wishing to do well, I afflict myself and lament.

Yet I take comfort that to my sombre self
—my night—has been conceded the sun clear and bright
Given to you at birth as your companion sent.

My Lady beauteous and kind
So much doth promise me
that merely seeing her, I find
Within my ancient tardy self
the Michelangelo once I was
Green and igneous of my youth
But now since envious death
Savagely sets himself between
My glances despairing and her's serene
Yet pity-brimmed
     Let suffice for me
that tiny interval of time when I am free
of death, and death I may obliterate
and take fire again and not abate.
But then sinister the thought with certain pace
Ever returns to its accustomed place
Where haughty ice doth quench the sweet fire
       and leaves no trace.

O rest assured, my eyes
        beyond surmise
that time flows
the hour nears
When the final step will shut the gate to tears
Now pity holds them open, nor will they close
Whilst my divine Lady
deigns on earth to dwell
If grace unlocks the sky
And draws her to itself anew
As it is wont as well
        for saints to do
then my living sun is gone,
Returned above and leaving me,
What's left then for my eyes to see?

If it be true
the soul, of its body unbound,
For some brief days and few
Returns to live and die once more upon this ground
Within some other body.
Will then my Lady
So infinitely lovely in my eyes
at her return, be then as now so cruel?
If my reasoning be wise
then I should expect in her new guise
a jewel: all kindness, unflawed with duress
For I believe that once her lovely eyes close,
With their reopening they must me caress
with pity of my dying once death she too knows.

[136]

Not only death but the mere fear of death
defends me and sets me free
from that lady lovely and iniquitous
who slays me unceasingly
and if at times the fire so calamitous
into which I fall
flares more than usual
No other remedy is there
than the image fixed at my heart's core
For where Death dwells Love draws not near.

If he who flees death and always sets aside
even the fear of it
Should leave it instead to orbit
in its own rounds and there abide,
then cruel love
in all its power would me prove
tenaciously tempering its dart
And pitilessly tear apart
a gentle heart.
But since the soul hopes to find its joy
elsewhere through death and ultimate grace
He who cannot fail but die
holds dear that very fear
beyond all others.
                        For that haughty lovely face
Extraordinary in its obdurance
No shelter provides against her stinging glance
No sanctuary against her disdain or bounty
O I swear to those who doubt this my saying
that, against her who laughs at my weeping,
And ever me has offended
Alone am I defended
And refuge tendered by annihilation:
For only she who slays me is my salvation.

Of a greater light, of a clearer star
Night illuminates its stars in the sky from afar
But you alone, from near, render by your mere vicinity
More beautiful all things less beautiful.
Which more—this or that—both bountiful
Can move or spur your heart to pity?
So that so long as mine doth blaze
At least yours doth not freeze?
Who, himself bereft, has granted you such bounty?
Such grace, such lovely forms, and all things fair,
Such face and eyes, such blond and shining hair?
Hence, against yourself (and me as well)
And to your own despite do you flee,
If beauty amidst the non-beautiful
Increases the beauty in itself to be.
Lady, if you should render up the dowers
Which heaven has granted you, and us deprived,
then less beautiful would be your face, more lovely ours.

Not without peril
is your divine face
for my soul nearing the place
of death. O too well
every hour
am I aware of that stalking power
whence I arm myself before I die
against the lovely encroachments you awake
But your kindness and your generosity
even while my end is so near
leaves me bereft of myself, and I fear
much less the price that one must pay
than the gifts you offer in exchange
For one does not change
the habits of many years in a single day.

In the lee of two beautiful lashes
Love regains its force
in that very season which scorns the bow and arrows
and their wingéd course dashes.
So my eyes, gluttonous for joys or sorrows,
whatever marvels are like yours
Makes trial of them, blessed or cursed,
in more than one fierce burst
So at the very heart of sweetness
                    am I assailed
by bitter overwhelming thoughts of death and shame
And yet my love does not forsake this game
Nor recoil from graver harms or fears
For one hour does not undo
                    the habits of many years

That my life might longer endure
the excess of ardor
Which deprives me of self
and then restores me to self
so that I fall or rise
according to the opening and closing of your eyes,
Magnets have they become
attracting me, my soul, whatever be my worth
in misery or mirth,
So that Love, listless and numb
hesitates, trembles, fears despite
all to kill me outright
Perhaps because it is blind
So that to penetrate my heart
since it is enchambered in yours
first yours it must find
and pierce those doors
wherein you and I are entwined
And since killing me would kill you
that it will not do.
O great martyrdom
Dolor-stricken, dumb
grief of mortality without dying
O double languishing, O double sighing!
Were I myself, I would be free;
   My own self cherish,
O give me back to myself that I may perish!

While my past persists within my present
As every hour I find,
O false world, then know I well and resent
the pains and faults of humankind
The heart which ultimately yields
to your flatteries, your vain delights, all the alluring fields
and secures but dolorous griefs for the soul,
O he who experiences the world knows and pays that toll,
How often have you promised others peace and goodness
that you had not to give and never did possess.
Hence he who sojourns longest here, less grace is given
For who lives least, more lightly-laden returns to heaven.

Time, no matter how you may constrain
me and spur me evermore with war
to render to the earth again
My afflicted limbs, my weary pilgrimage
Yet has not ended Love's barrage
        which the soul saddens
        and me gladdens
Nor does it seem that he will spare me
this locking and unlocking of my heart
        Now that I must depart
        Yet he will impair me
with doubts though the hour be close
And in that other life deprive me of repose
        For my habitual error
        Persists stronger every hour
        the more time effaces me,
        contains me, encases me.
O crueler than any other is my fate!
        For it is too late
To free myself of such anguish and fears,
For a heart which has flared and flamed so many years
Will, if reason water on it dashes
be reduced to no more a heart, but coal and ashes.

The accumulated years have brought me to this final hour
Too late, O world, do I know your delights.
Promises of peace not within your power
to render others, nor within your rights;
Repose which dies before it is born
      And so I should be torn
      by shame and fears
      to which heaven sets a term of years
And yet, instead, all that does in me awake
      My old and sweet mistake
Which kills the soul, nor benefits the flesh;
      thus all goes wrong
in one who lives too long.
This do I say, and of my own experience relate
And proclaim it with my own breath
For him alone heaven preserves a better fate
Who at his birth is closest to his death.

—Blessèd are you who in heaven enjoy
Tears which the world cannot compensate,
Does love try you still? Or do you employ
that freedom which death alone can liberate?

—Our eternal tranquility
is outside Time, hence we
love without envy.
Without anguish, caress

—therefore to my distress
Must I continue, as you see,
Living and loving, serving sorrow
to the bitter marrow?
If heaven be a friend to lovers forlorn
Why, loving, was I born
to live so long? O this causes me alarm
for a little is too much
for one who serves so willingly
and suffers such indignity and harm.

[146]

While my life flees through Time's sluice
Love destroys me evermore
Nor grants me an hour's truce
as I believed due after so many years.
Instead, my soul, tremulous, in tears
ceases not to roar
like a man unjustly dying
crying out
to me of his eternal damnation.
Thus, dangling in doubt
between fear and love's deception,
In the selfsame second I search out
the better of those two and choose the worser
Thus good counsel by bad usage is conquered
And all my fine intentions ever erred.

To Dante*

From Heaven he returned after he had seen
in his flesh the Hell of justice and pity's Purgatory
And thence alive returned to tell his story—
Thus, contemplating God and what that true light doth
    mean

He shed upon us all. O lucent star whose rays
mistakenly illumined the nest where I was born
O the wicked world entire would not suffice as his prize
Only Thou who has created him alone.

Of Dante I speak whose work and worth were thrust
aside, unrecognized by that ungrateful people while
they failed to grant their favors only to the just.

Were I but him! born to such fortune and fate
to confront with such virtue his bitter exile,
I would exchange the world's most happy state.

* See Notes 147-48

To Dante

How shall we praise him beyond praise?
For too blinded are we by his splendor
Easier to chastise all the more
the folks who flailed him than rise to his bays
—even the least—. For our benefit he displays
Just punishments, then back to God will soar.
Heaven opens for him but his country shuts the door
to his nostalgic yearning for accustomed ways.

O ungrateful, I say, feeding its own vices,
its own misfortune! Whence we clearly see:
to more perfect beings more griefs abound.

And among a thousand reasons this suffices:
Had he not been exiled unworthily
His like or greater would never have been found.

[149]

The soul overflows its hidden springs
Only that they may not extinguish the fire
Whereto it has converged entire,
And other help is vain, nothing brings the fire higher
Old and at-the-brink as I am.
                              Thus duress,
my harsh fate, fortune's adversity and sting
for all their painful tempering
                    yet do afflict me less
the more they emblazon me
So that your glances glowing
May set my tears flowing
And yet within are circumscribed, and in my soul
enwalled
So that which kills others, keeps me enthralled.
And I
By that alone live and take joy.

[150]

If you yield joys, O Love,
Only by toils and trials and tentatives most trying
then dear yet to me are arrows flying,
Which between death and dolor leave
no time whatever, nor the briefest space.
Whence I thank thee not for grief
                     but for the grace
only of death
which every ailment cures by loss of life and breath.

[151*]

Should the senses scatter
their too-hot ardor
Away from your fair face to some other face, O much less
power, my lord, does it possess,
like an impetuous Alpine torrent branched in two
So the heart which thrives most in more ardent flames
Adjusts but poorly to laments occasional and few
and luke-warm sighs and whimpering games.
the soul, of this error aware,
takes joy that one of them must die
that it might to heaven fly
whereto it has always yearned,
and there your martyrdoms are churned
And parceled out by reason, the firmest tempering whatever
all four concord in loving you forever.**

---

* This madrigal and the following were set to music by Arcadelt. See Notes
   151 and 152.
** 'all four' (*tutt'a quattro*) refer to Reason, the Senses, the Heart, the Soul.

1.

O tell me, Love, if the soul of this Lady
were as generous, as kind as her face is lovely?
Would anyone so stupid be
as not to deprive himself of himself,
                    himself blend
in her, give himself entirely to her?
And I—were she my friend—
How much more could I bestir
to serve her, love her
—my enemy! my foe!—
Whom I adore
more than I should, far more.

2.

O mighty gods, I say, by your command
Mankind should support adversity
No matter how or where, by sea, by land,
Only after death will you be
revenged of all your wrongs and injuries
                For then She
                loving thee
As now you burn for her felicities
She will your just vendetta bring
Alas! Alas! for one who waits
                    too late too late
that I arrive with comforting
But still
look we but well,
the generous noble heart commends
Pardon and loves her who offends.

He who does that which he should not do
Awaits — as the people say — in vain
Gratitude or just rewards due,
My felicity I thought rested in you
But this was not so: Again and again
Myself depriving of myself out of too much belief.
Nor do I hope to return reborn in the sun
as doth the phoenix. Time grants me no such boon.
And yet I take pleasure in my doleful grief
Because being yours I am more myself
than if I were exclusively myself.

No need had your exquisite soul
to tie me with a cord as I vanquished lay
        For if I well recall
a single glance sufficed to take me prey.
The weak heart, imprisoned, cannot
                abide or abate
prolonged pains, but swiftly must capitulate.
          But who would ever dream
              that taken prize
by your lovely eyes, within a mere few days
Dry burnt wood should sprout again to green?

[155]

So varied the effects, O my Lady,
of your grace and of my fate
that I must learn to negotiate
between the bitter and the sweet
Whatever destiny I greet
When inwardly benign you are, and kind
And outwardly your beauty feeds the fire
of my ardent desire
Yet my misfortune: bitter, blind
enemy of all our pleasures
Casts away such treasures
And with a thousand outrages my joy offends
But if instead of such martyrdom descends
good fortune to allay my passion
then would I be stripped of your compassion.
Thus, between laughter and tears, which so contrary are,
There is no mean to diminish my despair.

Of living stone alone
Art seeks here to perpetuate her face
As long as all Time
this being of my making, my handiwork of stone
What will Heaven create of her, sublime,
                    that nothing can efface?
Since this is mine and that His creation
Not simply mortal but divine,
Not only in my eyes and estimation
And yet it disappears and lasts but little time.
Read aright its future is uncertain
Limping out of sight
O that a rock should remain
while she without stain
Death hastily removes!
Who then shall take vendetta? O
                    it behooves
on Nature alone, since of all she does create
Our works last but hers disintegrate.

That your astounding beauty in this world
might be embodied in a creature less cruel
—a gentler lady—. Let nature's rule
be reversed, I pray. Let all your loveliness
which day by day declines and grows less,
be reclaimed, and serve to refashion
of your face so serene, without compassion
a figure more kind under celestial signs.

And let to love be assigned perpetual care
to refill your heart with benevolence,
And let my sighs and my tears be gathered there,
And given to one born then whom she might love perchance.
So, perhaps moved by my grief she will bestow
upon a stranger what to me she will not show.

This is no time, O Love, for my heart to be enflamed
Or take joy or terror at mortal beauty's dower
For now has arrived the final hour
When one with little left is ashamed
And grieves all the more the time lost, the wasted perturbations.
Death makes a fool of great infatuations
No matter how much you give me, within your arm's equipoise
Death mocks at such great blows
And the more that which should not, greens and grows
the more it is leveled:
                              my talents and my words
Enflamed by you to my misfortune
Are turned to water, made absurd
No matter how I may importune
For God would have it now that into that pool
Should flow all the sins of this old fool.

—For many, Lady★, indeed for a thousand lovers
Were you, of angelic form, created.
Now one alone has appropriated★★
What to so many were given
So that it seems asleep is heaven.

O lighten our laments and cries
With the sunshine of your eyes!
that seem to scorn
to grant that gift where such unhappiness is born.

—O disturb not your sacred desires
for he who, it seems, but aspires
to despoil you, deprive you of me
will not enjoy felicity.★★★
For great fear unpleasures great sin
And among lovers, less felicitous are those
Whose great desire is curbed by the very throes
of great fulfillment.
                              Far happier who grope
lost in misery but full of hope.

★ On the autograph del Riccio wrote: "According to messer Michelangelo
Buonarroti, the Lady symbolizes the city of Florence." The poem is there-
fore a political dialogue between the Florence exiles (first part) and the
response of the city (in the second part).

★★ A reference to the tyrannical Alessandro de' Medici, appointed Duke of
Florence in 1532.

★★★ Indeed, he did not enjoy felicity very long. Alessandro was assassinated
in 1537 by his cousin, Lorenzino, Michelangelo subsequently carved in
honor of Lorenzino a bust of Brutus, the classic tyrannicide.

Laden with the years and after many trials
searching, the wise man, nigh to death, arrives
through harrowing of hives
where fantasy beguiles
      at the living image alone
      in alpine and enduring stone.
For too late, alas, does one attain lofty new ideas.
      too little time is ours
      too few moments remain.
So with Nature it is the same time and again,
In this face or that, erring often, often failed
Now that the topmost peak is scaled
—Sheer loveliness!—and there is your divine face!
O then he too is old, about to die
      in that high and icy place
Whence the fears; that death and beauty
      are inextricably woven.
On such strange food, in such a pasture strange
      does my desire range
And crop and nourish me and I am cloven
For, you beheld, I know not if portend
Joys or griefs, delight or the universe's end.

Not always does everyone appreciate
that which contents the senses.
                              Nor is it rare
that someone should berate
What others hold dear, finding foul fair
And bitter what to others seems sweet
                              and victory defeat.
Good taste is so rare
that to the mistaken many it feigns to yield
                  While behind the shield
of self it takes pleasure
according to its own values and measure.
Thus, losing, I harvest and glean
What from without is not seen;
Who saddens my soul and does not hear its sighs.
the world is blind and its judgments or praise
Most satisfy those who wish it least
like a whip which teaches and tears like a beast.

If sometimes, emerging from the hard stone,
the image of all others resembles oneself,
Often gloomy, unkempt, wan
Do I make her as she has made me
And it seems that when I think to carve her alone
My model is myself, my example ever me.
Well then might I groan
that the rough resistant stone
In which her image lies
Resembles her, nor can I otherwise
Destroyed and mocked by her
But sculpt my own afflicted members
Yet if the future remembers
What art chooses to endure
then happy let her make me, sure,
And beautiful will I shape her.

Humbly my neck I yield to the bitter yoke,
My face beaming at its atrocious fate,
Nor does my faithful fiery heart abate
In love for my enemy, my mistress
But rather every hour fear my grief grow less
For if your face serene pastures my distress,
Feeds my martyrdom, lends it breath,
What cruel pain then can cause me Death?

More comely and less kind
An outward semblance than yours, my Lady,
Is nowhere to be found
No other soul so sweetly, so profound
Pulses in a will and mind
Ungrateful for your beauty's gift
And so deserving perpetual pains of Hell
More than I, bereft,
Deserve Heaven for my sufferings
And all the slings and all the bufferings
I neither say it nor will conceal it
Whether I yearn or do not yearn
that my sin be like your sin
And I, like you, endure the burn
And the waters that anneal it
If not in life than in death
to be where you will be — that blazing heath
Or should you pity show
then will I blessèd go
As martyrs do to my eternal peace
and if Hell with you be sweet
What then would Heaven be?
                A doubly blessèd seat
Where I alone amidst the Divine Choir
One Lord in Heaven and one on earth adore.

Because your trust in me, O Lady
by contrast with my hope
        —a lofty aspiration—
   is of brief duration
Should I regard you with a healthy disillusioned eye
then will I savor for what it is
                all those promises
latent in your eyes
—illusions, lies—
No matter. Even without pity
Pleasure is wrought by boundless beauty
And though I sense within thee
effects contrariwise
to the mercy of your eyes
I tempt not certainty
But pray that where enjoyment be less than complete
At least doubt is sweet
to one whom truth only brings brambles and stings.

Now in this chill season
of my age no longer green
Still flares beyond all reason
the flame unspent, if lean.

thus Love who doth remember
that aimed at a gentle heart
the blow hits true, ignites the ember,
And so he draws with art

His bow . . . and all is green again!
Green green the dry place!
At the merest glimpse of a lovely face
Green the bark and green the fen!

And this ultimate arrow, barbed, astounding,
brings me down to a second Fall
More painful than my first wounding
More dolorous, dangerous than them all.

O how fleeting every hour
the days remaining yet to me
Fire contained hath greater power
to disadvantage, damage me
Time dwindles and confines the flame
to my grave punishment and pain
    And help from heaven
    is not given
to guard me in this brief balance left
Against my former inclinations
    and so I am bereft
    and begirt with damnations
Yet you are not content
to have locked me within
    this encirclement of sin
    this circumscribed flame
where even rocks cannot maintain
their nature, not to speak of a heart
And so I thank thee, Love, for your kind intent
Since less invincible, my heart
lasts not long within a closed fire
    consumed upon that pyre
The worse is my good fate instead
for living exposed to the arms you bear
life to me is no more dear
and you grant at least your pardon to the dead.

O I outdo myself: pledging in advance
        lofty concepts, noble propositions —
        even the time promising and the conditions
to realize what neither fate nor chance
holds in reserve for me, nor I deserve.
O foolish thoughts, vain and drear
                for with death so near
I lose the present and the future's wrenched from me
And yet I hope to cure my malady
burning for your countenance's grace.
So, dead, I live by that face
                dreaming still to thrive
in those very years where life does not arrive.

If she takes pleasure in my laments
And you too, Love,
My miseries approve,
Pasturing only on my complaints.

If I, like thee,
Am so accustomed grown to nurture my life
On tears, anguish, ice, strife
Then deprived would I be
of life itself were she
to profess
unwonted mercy, gentleness.

O better far would be the worst!
Contrary foods cause contrary effects
For I would be curst
with loss of life and she of pleasure
Should you, Love, deprive me of my treasure
—her cruelty—which to my joy she elects.
The more you offer to relieve my pain
the more you promise death again.
For, the anguished soul
in its tormented toil
Prefers far more to live under fate's mallet blows
than enjoy the grace which death alone bestows.

Not only does the empty mold
Await to be filled with silver or with gold
Conquered by fire.
But to bring forth the work entire
the mold must be broken.

Such am I: the fires of love unspoken
Still blazing within, and my desires in duress
empty yet of the infinite loveliness
of her whom I adore
in my most secret core:
Body and soul of my fragile life
Lofty Lady
who descends into me
through passages so brief
Such narrow spaces and means
that to bring her forth
I must be shattered to smithereens.

So much above myself
O Lady do you cause me to rise
that I know not how to say it, or surmise
or even what to think, for flesh still clings
though I am no longer myself.

Whence if you lend me your wings
Why do I not more often soar
And fly to your legendary face
And there in that holy place
With thee remain and thee adore
Since Heaven thus concedes
                    that one may rise
with all one's mortality to Paradise?

        And yet and yet it needs
be said that by the fortune of your grace
I may from my soul be sundered
        (O endless-to-be-wondered-
at miracle beyond breath!)
that fleeing to thee, with thee, flees Death.

Those tormenting glances on others wasted
Rob me entirely
of all I have not tasted.
And yet it is not theft
that I be bereft
You do not give away but what is yours.

But if the vulgar folk out of doors,
in every piazza, church
Seize it and it besmirch
And bespoil me beside,
That would be homicide.
For nigh to death by now would I be pressed.
Love, why then do you pardon all the rest?
And me alone deny
Your ultimate courtesy?

O fashion her anew beyond doubt
So kindly within, so ugly without
that she would fall in love with me
but would to me displeasing be.

[173]

O Love, Death hunts you out of me
        Scorns my sorrows
         Where once triumphantly
Not only with your bow and arrows
But even nude you held the field.
          Now, with proud ice congealed,
He suffocates the sweetness of those flames
        flaring now their few and final tongues.

In every heart virile and mature
Love prevails less, nor will endure.
And though one day you reached me on your wings
         Now all youthful things
          Flee from me in fears
For at this brink one only loathes the green years.

Because that half of me which comes from heaven
Returns there on broad wings of desire,
the other half remaining here to admire
a woman of loveliness unparalleled
        by whom I am compelled
to freeze and burn at once, driven
        by contrarieties;
And in such polarities
suspended: the one half of me doth steal
from the other
the good that should remain entire.

But if some day she should change her style
And half of me beguile
of the other half. And all my thoughts,
        scattered and weary, aspire
and converge upon her alone thronging,
And she then yield to my longing,
My soul will be hunted out of heaven
And I of half myself be riven
Yet then at least I hope to be
not hers by half, but entirely.

Epitaph for the Tomb of
Faustina Mancini Attavanti

Living still in us, here lies the divine
beauty seized by death before her time.
Had she with her right hand herself defended
She would have survived. But left-handed, thus ended.*

---

* Epitaph for Gandolfo Porrino, a poet from Mantova, in memory of a
woman whom he had loved, Fausta Mancini (left-handed) who died in
1543. The epitaph and the following sonnet were written by Michelangelo
in response to three sonnets which Porrino had sent him, the first praising
the Last Judgment and the other two asking the artist for a portrait of the
woman, either in painting or marble.

Michelangelo's Reply to Porrino's Request for a Portrait of La Mancina

The new lofty beauty which I consider
Unique in heaven as on this savage iniquitous earth
(The vulgar folk, blind, did not her worth
adore, and dubbed her Left-Handed as a slur.)

She was born but for you; I know not how, try as I may
to carve her into stone or with a pen sketch her rebirth.
Not in such images could I hope to quench your dearth
Which only her living lovely face reborn can allay.

And if as every other star
is conquered by the sun, so our intellect
should weigh now her worth of no less estimate.

Hence to your comfort, her new beauty afar
is shaped by God amongst the loftiest Elect,
And that, He alone, not I, can create.*

---

* See previous note. Michelangelo's adroit refusal utilizes the same rhyme
  scheme as Porrino's request; hence, it is a reply 'per le rime'. Hopefully, the
  mannered courtesy of the refusal would soften the hurt.

Of my ardor and of my flames
She is ever playing games
though she seems to lavish pity
her heart the while doth savage me.
Love, have I not often told you this?
She would never yield me bliss
And he who rests his hope upon another's boon
loses all that is his own.
But if she wishes me to perish
mine the fault, and mine the blemish
For I did lend her faith to my own harm
And she is guiltless that I believed her charm.

Scattering the sparks of great beauty
an ardent fire may ignite a thousand hearts.
Yet as a heavy stone, falling, hits
but a single man, kills one alone
while to the multitude is light as down
                    harmless and feathery.
                    So it is with me.
Just as flames enclosed in a small space
will pulverize and reduce
the hardest stone to lime
which water then dissolves in a tick of time
As well he knows who has discerned the truth
and tested it in life.
Thus have I become a conflagration
set by this divine girl
beset by her until a thousand tongues of flame curl,
flicker and play without cessation
in my heart's innermost chambers!
But if eternal tears quench those embers
And dissolve that which once was hard and strong
Then I do not long
for surcease: better to be nothing, lacking breath
than burn burn burn without death.

In the memory of beautiful things
Death must not come to deprive that very memory of his face
as it has deprived you of him, leaving no trace.
If fire becomes ice and laughter inevitably brings
tears, so death instills in us
such hatred of loveliness
that no more is it sovereign
over the hollow heart. But if to our surprise
somehow again should reign
　　　　　　　　those beautiful eyes
in their familiar frame
O dry wood will blaze in an ardent flame!

To the height of your lucent diadem
through steep and tortuous ways
No one O lady arrives to sing your praise
Whom you do not first endow with humility
                        which is the stem
                        of flowering courtesy.
For steeper the ascent, weaker is my strength
And my vigor fails me midway up the path
And yet that your beauty so supernal lies
Seems to render to my heart but delight and surprise
for greedily it yearns to climb
wherever there is rarity sublime

And yet do I wish you might descend
where I might attain to your loveliness
and thus enjoying it, put an end
to this toil and this distress.
In this thought am I satisfied:
If I presage your disdain and your pride
that in loving you low and hating you high
                        I have been
guilty, yet you will pardon yourself for my sin.

Indomitable, savage
this woman would ravage
me, determined I should burn, die, disintegrate
for that which by weight
counts less than an ounce
and my blood quart by quart
she sucks from my veins: unfibres me, aborts
My body from my soul.
O the joy she takes in this toll!
Making up before her faithful mirror, she sees
herself equal to Paradise
then turning to me, sullies my every fold
So that simply by being old
My face makes hers more beautiful.
                    Whence have I decided
the more am I derided
for being ugly, yet that is my
                    great fortune, special feature
For increasing her beauty I conquer nature.

If I had been in my earliest years aware
of fire, then from without, what now burns within,
I would have extinguished it that I might spare
my soul of this blow and this sin
and this weak heart which now is dead.
But from this earliest error derives instead
lifelong guilt, O unhappy soul, if in one's first hours
    against love one cowers
and poorly has oneself defended
Now in these final days when youth is ended
One still burns and dies of that distant blaze
    And those youthful ways
For he who cannot but be shaken
And in his green age taken
though now there be light and mirror,
    O weary, old
    me behold:
One much more easily destroyed by a minor fire.

Lady, though I be old and grave,
to you I return and re-enter
as the weight to its center
Outside of which no other peace I have.

Heaven holds forth the key.
Love turns it; twists it round
Opening her bosom to the just,
                    and forbidding me
iniquitous depraved desires (as she must)
and lifting me — weary, vile — off the very ground
to where the rare and semi-gods are found
From her graces descend
            Strange and sweet and pure
So that whoever dies for her
            Lives for himself at the end.

[184]

When I am with you, Lady
Sweetly O so kindly
from the heart spilling
spirits of renewal are instilling
life in the farthest reaches of my flesh,
Whence that mesh
of wants which is my soul
Impeded in its natural course
by that unexpected burst of joy, in remorse
departs forthwith; and I am no more whole.
Body and soul
shattered by the bitterness of your departure.
When, to my mortal aid, return
those very spirits to reflood the heart again
and overflow its chambers.
Then if I see thee
returning once again to me
I feel expelled once more
from the heart's core.
Whence torment and cure are equally cursed
And the middle path
for one who loves too much,
is always worst.

Love, it seems I find
so powerful your persuasion
You expel even death from my mind
and by that very kindness create confusion
in my soul which without such merciful intent
would be more content.

Fallen is the fruit and dry the bark
And that once sweet, now bitter is and stark,
        or at least appears to be.
        And still alone tormenting me
at this final brief hour
is infinite pleasure in a brief space —
        a dwindling bower.
Yes, I am simply terrified
by the pity in your face,
Your tardy powerful pity which undoes my pride
And is death to my body
        and bedevils my delight.
And yet in my fright
I thank you much, at any rate,
for if, at this age and of such a fate
I die, you have achieved my death
            —that ultimate distress—
not by death but rather kindliness.

That I, O noble Lady, less unworthy might
be of the gift of your immense courtesy
When first I encountered it, I thought to employ
my humble talent with all my heart for your delight.

But then I realized to rise to that height
One's own genius does not open the way
And pardon do I beg for my gross audacity
Each hour wiser grown in failure's light

And I see well how faulty to believe
that the grace which divinely rains from you, may
like my works be time-stricken and frail.

For genius and art and memory yield to it and leave
no trace. Not even a thousand mortal efforts can repay
that one single gift which is celestial.

Draggingly to death
as one justly condemned to the gallows
not otherwise do I face my end
where soul flutters free, where breath
chokes, obliterates all powers
so close to me is death
Save that more closely come, more slowly pass the
hours.

Yet, Love, not even in this state
Do you abate
your tyranny
permitting me
to live one hour peacefully
between two perils.
Whether I sleep or vigil keep
Hope humble, double-pronged, quarrels
with fate so that weary and old
I either burn or grow more cold
Nor do I know
Whether more harm or less doth hope bestow
But still I fear thee more, Love, whose glances
slay more swiftly the later fly those lances.

Were you less kind, less grace on me bestow
the more certain would be my salvation
     though fewer tears would flow
     down my breast between both banks of my eyes.
Yet you would keep me still alive and wise
So your benevolence diminished doubles,
outshadows and annuls those tiny bubbles
of my virtues, pricks them to annihilation.

Nor does the wise man ever desire
(unless he spur himself)
joys beyond his worth
for all excess is vain, indeed insane
And the man simple and plain by birth,
Modest, of humble fortune, knows more tranquility.

O Lady, that which to you may be permitted, will
hardly prove helpful to me though I have been selected.
For giving others what others never expected
Can of excess pleasure only kill.

I cannot but be lacking in genius and in art
     compared with her
Who deprives me of life by the excess
of her kindness which kills the heart.
Such help I would bless
all the more were it less.
Whence my soul must depart
    as the eye is injured
    by one who radiates such splendor.

Thus, above me she transcends
    beyond my possibilities.
No hope to me portends
nor does she
   —Lady lofty and serene
    beyond any earthly queen—
lift me to the skies
to make me equal to the least of her gifts.
So that I must learn: who lifts
Also lowers, for I am unworthy of my guide
and she with me cannot be satisfied.
And yet so full of grace is she
    (O here's the riddle!)
So abounding, she sets others aflame
    with a fire bounded,
For too-much burns with less heat than too-little.

If vulnerable I was from my earliest years
    so that the tiniest flame, ardor's merest dart
    did swiftly consume my green heart.
What now when an insatiable fire sears
A heart often burnt in the enclosured fears
    of these ultimate hours? If to the remaining part
    of life, dying in strength, valor, art
the amorous conflagration again appears?

O it will make of me what I expect:
    Ashes in the wind: ferocious, piteous
    Purging my body of those wearisome worms.

For if in youth I burnt green and erect
    to a flicker of flame, now dry, declined,
    what will the igneous
    fury do to my soul as this old body warms?

If by fire alone can the smith extend
and shape the iron to the concept in his mind.
Nor without flame can gold be refined
and by the artist wrought to beauty's end.

Nor will the unique phoenix be resurrect
if not first burnt; whence I burning dying,
Purer do I hope to resurge amongst those flying
in death reborn whom time cannot offend or select.

The fire of which I speak is still given
to place its hearth in me for my renewal
since now I'm almost numbered among the dead.

If by nature fire soars to heaven,
its proper sphere, and I become the fuel
and flames, must they not bear me too at their head?

So friendly is the inner fire to the cold stone
that drawn therefrom, contained, it will pulverize
the rock, embraced in flame, which in another guise
lives forever, binding others to itself alone.

And if hardened in the kiln wherein it's thrown,
It will conquer winter and summer, and be more praised
    than before,
As purged, the soul will from Hell to Heaven soar
to dwell with other souls near God's throne.

So it is with me; If I am undone
by the fire which plays hidden within me, I must
be burnt to ashes that I may more life enfold.

Since if I live, made all of smoke and dust,
Fire-inured I will endure forever as one
Not by iron forged but by gold.*

* See Introduction p. xii.

If joyous heart beautifies a face
and an unjoyous one uglifies it
And if a woman beautiful and cruel
such effects does trace,
             What signifies it?
             Who will she be
who burns not for me as I for her?
And since my eyes were born
under a guiding star
Sharply to discern
beautiful from beautiful
distinguishing their every subtlety,
then no less cruel is she
against herself as against me.
For so often do I say —
Regard this face of mine. Ah, you start!
But it derives from a grimaced heart! —
Since we depict ourselves in others.
Then painting a woman how shall we render her
If she makes us disconsolate?
And it were well for us both —
             She in youth and I in age —
Could I portray her with a happy heart
             and dry visage
O then felicity!
Making her beautiful and myself not ugly.

For that, O Lady, which I see of you from without
However much the truth pass not to the eye
I hope my weary cast-down thoughts might sometimes flout
the inner essence and enjoy repose
in what I see
though flesh be not clothes.
For the more I know the worst of your inwardness
the worse will grow my distress.
If your heart harbors cruelty
While your lovely eyes promise me
                true consolation
              for my lamentation—
O that would be the time!
When honest love scorns the sublime
And hopes for nothing more and nothing more protests
than outward semblance manifests.
Lady, if your soul
be truly contrary to your eyes
that is no surprise
I will pay that toll
For even against that cheat
Do I take pleasure in a lovely dame's deceit.

O fountains! O rivers! let my eyes flow again
with the waves of a deep-rooted spring
Cresting higher, impetuously pulsing
More than is your nature to attain.

And you, air humid with my agony,
My melancholy eyes, my sighing —
      all this tempering
with celestial light. O to my heart bring
serenity and to my vision accuity

that I may sharply see your somber face serene
O return my pacing to the earth that grass again may grow.
and re-tune Echo, now deaf to my lament

And reclaim those sacred scintillations I have seen
that I might another beauty know
Since you are clearly not with me content.

How can it be, O Lady, as anyone may see
by long experience, that the image longer lives
in alpine hard stone then he who gives
it life? the bust endures, the artist will be

reduced to ashes. So cause yields to effect
Whence art is victorious over nature,
As I who carve beautiful statues do aver
Since the artwork Time and Death do not affect.

Hence I may to both of us long life assign
by whatever means, either in color or stone
Seeming our very faces, yours or mine.

So that a thousand years after we have gone
the world will see how beautiful you were
And I pathetic, yet not stupid in loving her.

When your lovely eyes turn,
Lady, and glance closely into mine
    then I do discern
      in your eyes myself as you yourself in mine.
Reduced by age and punishment
All that I am is mirrored there
      While mine reflect you fair and far
      More luminous than a lucent star.
Perhaps this is heaven's judgment
that in your lovely eyes I see myself so ugly
      And no less savage and cruel
      is Reason which the eyes rule
and judicates that through them you penetrate
      and harbor in my heart
Whilst you lock me out and set me apart
      For the seige of an inferior
      Only inures your worth superior
And this is the sad truth
that love requires parity and youth.

[199]

With a heart of sulphur, flesh of tow
Bones of dry wood, soul without compass
or bridle, open to desire's excess,
Blind to reason, weak, stumbling, slow

to the traps and deceits the world doth show —
it is no wonder that at the tiniest caress
of the first spark, I take fire, and bless
the very conflagration into which I go.

For if I was born, not deaf or blind, to outdo nature
with that art which heaven has bestowed
and entrapped and enrapt in its allure

then my heart combustible must be allowed
its vulnerability and let fall the blame
on that one who cast me in the flame.

Since you are in my heart, I evaluate
myself of higher worth than usual,
As marble intaglio'd by my chisel
is worth far more than in its rough state.

Or as paper written on, or folio painted, will rate
higher, more esteemed than a common wrinkled rag.
Thus am I, since I have become the flag
and target of your glances, whose blows I do not hate.

So stamped, imprinted I saunter everywhere and find
myself secure as one armed, or with talismans, chosen
against whatever perils or traps of desire.

I prevail against water or against fire,
Marked by you I re-illuminate the blind,
And with my saliva cure whatever poison.

If the soul, at the Final Day, returns
to its sweet desired flesh
           Hosanna'd or grieved
           As is believed
Either saved in heaven or damned where one burns
Eternally,
Hell will be
less dolorous for me
If it be adorned by your loveliness.
           Thus rather than mourned
We may your beauty celebrate
So long as others contemplate
and gaze at you.
           But if instead
it rise to heaven and there reside
As I in dread and pride
for both our souls desire
in all solicitude and warm affection,
Then less will I take joy in the contemplation
of God, and less will I aspire,
Since there as here below
All pleasures take second place
Yielding to your sweet face.
Therefore I hope to love you better where I go
Since to the damned, less grief softens the sting,
So those in Heaven are not harmed by a lesser blessing.

Now on my right foot, now on my left,
Shifting so, I seek my salvation
between virtue and vice in desperation
My heart confused, bereft
travails me, assails me
like one who sees no heaven
And whose every path is lost and riven.
So I offer you this blank page
On which you may write in holy ink
Disillusioning me
of love's illusions and rage
And of truth alone make me to think
And by your piety
Set my soul of itself free
that it no longer shall entangled be
in our mortal errors and terrors
in the brief time remaining me —
This, O Lady, lofty and divine,
tell me: does heaven assign
to a repentant sinner a lower storey
than to the supremely good in all their glory?

With every hour the more I hate myself and flee,
So much the more to thee,
Lady, with true hope do I turn.
And the less my soul fears for me
the closer you are, for whom I yearn;
All heaven's promises and revelation
Shining in your face, your eyes brimming with my salvation
And often am I well aware,
On others gazing everywhere,
that heartless eyes are virtue-less eyes
O luminaries beyond satiety!
O lights blazing like the sun!
Nor to be seen less than desire would aspire
For seeing them infrequently
is nigh to oblivion.

My eyes in love with beautiful things,
My soul thirsting for salvation,
possess no other power that brings
them to heaven but the contemplation
of all that is beautiful,
From the highest stars stream down a splendor
that draws desire to the full
And that is the wonder
that here on earth is called Love.
      To rise above
itself, no other means hath a gentle heart
Nor other counsel impart
but to become enamoured, burn,
        learn love's avatars
from that face whose eyes resemble stars.

Overwhelming grace, O Lady, like overwhelming grief
Kills equally, as when a thief facing the final price,
Deprived of hope, his veins rivers of ice,
Should suddenly be freed, beyond belief.

Thus if your kindness should grant relief
More than is your wont; and with excessive pity
Soothe my tribulations and my misery,
This it seems would, more than tears, truncate my life.

So it occurs with bitter-sweet news;
Their contrarieties bring death in an instant
When the heart contracts and expands excessively.

So if your beauty, sustained by love and heaven, choose
To keep me alive, then curb my content,
For weak virtue dies of too much gratuity.

Sometimes my hope might well be unfurled
and rise together with desire and yet not prove in vain,
For if heaven is displeased with every pulse of pain,
then to what end did God create the world?

And what reasons more just for loving you
than to glorify that peace perpetual
Whence descends the divine in you, and the eternal,
And every heart makes chaste approving you.

Only that love is tainted which false hope impels,
And every moment dies with beauty's diminution,
Subject so to a fair face's variation.

But sweet that love which in a modest heart dwells,
Nor diminishes with the skin's changing attire
Or at the final hour, here will Paradise acquire.

If long delay reaps more grace and fortune
than that which normally attends desire,
mine, so late, torments me and casts me in the mire
for the joys of an old man have brief duration.

For heaven is opposed, if it heeds us at all,
that we burn at a time when we should freeze;
As I do for this woman; hence tears provide no ease
Since they are weighted with the years that hold me in thrall.

But perhaps, although we are at end of day:
the sun sunken almost beyond the horizon
Amongst frigid shadows and dense weirs

If love enflames us only in the middle of our years,
Nor is it otherwise, then if I'm old yet blaze within,
It is a woman converts my end into midway.

As I have borne for some time in my mind
the image, Lady, of your face printed there,
        Now that I find
        Death drawing near
With permission granted Love should imprint upon the soul.
So that from this terrestrial jail
felicitous be its departure
from the heavy cadaver.
In tempest or in calm
Safely stamped with such a seal
like the sign of the Cross against its adversaries,
the soul might to heaven return
Where nature did steal you away
that you might exemplary be
to the splendid angels that they learn
to create anew for the world in that lofty place
An involucre of flesh that will replace
the departed spirit of your beautiful face.

Though beauty be divine and resides in the celestial sphere,
Yet it manifests itself in your human face here,
    Lady, such distant pleasure
    Provides me short measure
So that I never cease to gaze upon your human face.
     Since for my soul in pilgrimage
     fixed upon your fair visage,
Every other path is steep and narrow
and no other choice does it allow.
    Thus I divide my time
    (hardly sublime):
Daylight for my eyes, night for my heart:
No interval wherein I might aspire to heaven.
    Without alleviation or leaven
My destiny at birth
Fixes me upon your splendor on earth
Nor permits my fervent feelings to rise
If nothing else there be
    which draws us to the skies,
the mind to heaven, for grace, misericordia
           or clemency;
Late loves the heart what the eye does not see.

Returning whence it issued forth for humankind
the immortal form like an angel flew
into your earthly prison, its grace to bestow,
Honoring the world and curing the mind.

Of this alone am I enamored, to all else blind,
Not only of your face serene from an outward view,
O not only in this which must decline anew
does love place faith nor there virtue find.

Only thus, lofty new things out of nature arise
And heaven is generous with her gifts at their birth
to all the teeming creatures of this earth

And nowhere does God in his grace reveal his paradigm
more clearly to me that in some human guise
And that alone I love because it mirrors Him.

* Final poem of the del Riccio collection.

If some part of a woman be beautiful
though the others be ugly
Must I love them all
for the great pleasure afforded me by that one alone?
the part which appeals to, and is by reason approved,
while it makes of joy a melancholy
Yet would have it that my innocent folly
be excused, nay, even loved.
But Love, as if enraged
at the irritating sight
is wont to cry out with all his might:
In his realm one cannot be engaged
in such appeals, and to such expectations turn
And heaven itself would have it that I yearn
So that pity for the displeasing not be a vain affliction,
For familiar seeing cures every imperfection.

Love, if you're a god,
Can't you do as you wish? as you would?
O do for me then, if you can
What I would do for thee
if I were Love, and not a mere man.
Unsuitable is great desire,
Unfit the hope to aspire
toward lofty beauty. Even more
the consequences. Even more
vain for one at death's door
O heed my request!
And let your satisfaction rest in my bequest.
Can sweetness be
in what oppresses me?
Can I enjoy what would me efface?
Do not a few hours of grace
but double the martyrdom?
            to this point have I come
And this more would I say:
What will death be, I pray,
if to the miserable it is cruel,
        then what will it be
for one who dies at the very summit of felicity?

Singular and new, this woman's beauty
Spurs me, unbridles me, whips me
And not only have sounded the canonical clanging
of tierce, but nones and vespers,
                          and soon it is evening.
My birth and my destiny,
One playing with death
Nor can the other give me
Entire peace here on earth
I, who was accustomed
to my white head and old age
and already held in hand the pledge
of another life, its certainty assumed,
promised by a contrite heart.
But he who fears the least, loses the most,
in the ultimate voyage to an unknown coast,
trusting in his own valor and art
against the familiar passion
of Love's uproarious ocean
And if memory remains but in the ears,
Without grace, what profits the years?

That no more need we cull together
from many to make one
Beauty complete and entire
beyond which was none,
All was lent to a Lady lofty and sincere
clad in the purest veil
But to redeem this loan would fail
all the world, I fear,
and poorly reimburse Heaven.
But now in a brief gasp
Rather, in a second, God did grasp
her to his bosom, quite indifferent
to the world and its surprise
that she has been taken from our eyes
Removed from this firmament.
But though her flesh be dead
her sweet pious lovely verse instead
cannot be forgotten.
Thus is proved the cruelty of pity:
If Heaven bestowed such loveliness
upon the ugly as a loan
and now redeemed them by death alone,
We would all die in distress.

What marvel is it, if close to the fire
I melted and burned; and now that it is spent
from without, from within I am afflicted and rent
and bit by bit reduced to ashes of a perished pyre?

Burning I used to see the source of my desire,
the lucent place whence depended my torment.
That sight alone lent me content
And death and dole to me were festivals and gyre.

But when the splendor of that incendiary food
that burnt me and nurtured me flew off to heaven
One coal though covered, yet remained glowing.

And if love heap not up other wood
to set me aflame, not a single spark even
will remain of me, all to cinders and ashes going.

Here am I enclosed like dough within the crust,
like a genie bottled in an ampule
Here I live poor and alone in the dust.

And my dark tomb's a short flight wide, miniscule,
where Arachne and her thousand workmen and assistants
weave a bobbin of themselves from stool to stool.

Around my door are piles of giants' excrement
Since those who gobble grapes or have taken medicine
go nowhere else to shit to their full content.

I've also learned to recognize the urine
and the tube it squirts from into the pit
which summons me each morning at dawn-shine.

Cats, carrion, birds, bedpans of shit
left there for housekeeping or to shorten a journey,
No one ever comes to clean my things, without a deposit.

My soul has such an advantage over my body
that if, unclogged, it should assuage the stink
Neither bread nor cheese could contain it truly.

Only coughing and cold keep me from dying, I think,
And if my breath does not escape from that lower exit
then it can scarcely issue from the mouth's chink.

Split, shattered, ruptured and vexèd
am I already through fatigue, and the hostelry
is Death, where I live and eat as the landlord recks it.

My jollity is my melancholy
and my repose resides in these woes
Whoever looks for trouble, God grants a-plenty.

At the Feast of the Magi those
Who see me there see me truly and apart.

Better yet to see my house midst sumptuous palaces and
    shows.

No flame of love remains within my heart
And if a greater grief always drives out a lesser
Every feather have I plucked and shaven from my soul lest
    it depart.

A hornet buzzes in my skull as in a jar.
My bones and marrow I keep inside a leathern sack.
And in a bowl three pills of pitch are.

My eyes are ground and pestled pale lilac,
My teeth like keys of an instrument
at whose touch my voice speaks or does not speak.

My face the very form of fear has, and torment.
My clothes, with no other rags, serves as a scarecrow
to chase away the crows from the dry seeds and firmament.

In one ear a spiderweb is stretched below.
In the other a cricket sings all night.
Gasping with catarrh I cannot sleep, or snore like the
    scirocco.

Love, the muses, grottoes flowering and bright—
My scribbles serve as dunce-caps or tamborines
for innkeepers, latrines, or ladies of the night.

Why did I want to make such puppets by the lot?
What was the use if they have brought me to this end?
Like one who crossed the sea, then drowned in snot.

My art so praised, and once so honored, did defend
me once; but now has brought me to this boon:
A poor old man, I serve others and to their power bend

So that I am undone, if I die not soon.

Since age steals away
desire, though I am deaf and blind
I am at peace with death, I find:
weary, nearing the final saying, the final day.
The soul that fears and adores
What the eye does not see
worships yet abhors,
distances me, O Lady, from your lovely face
as from a perilous and charming place.
Love which does not yield to truth, but ever yearning
once more fills my heart with fiery burning
and seems to say to me:
loving is no human thing . . .

[218]

Now with icy pride, now ardently ablaze,
Now with years and woes and shame laden and armed,
I mirror with sad and dolorous hope all my days:
the future in the past
the good which did not last
the evil which distresses me,
Afflicts me, oppresses me—
Of whatever fortune: joyful or adverse,
Every hour I ask forgiveness; the propitious or perverse
are weary of me already.
I see all too well
that good luck and grace
reside in life's brevity.
One moment can efface
many years of hell.
Since life is all fugacity
and death's the sovereign medicine for misery.

[219]

You always give me out of your left-overs
And ask of me things that are not.*

* The meaning as well as person addressed in this autonomous diptych is
obscure. It is found on the reverse of the same sheet bearing the two
preceding madrigals.

[220]

I have been, O Love, for many years now
with you and by you nourishing my soul
And not entirely, my body too
and with admirable art, hopeful desire made me whole.

But now, alas, wingèd thought soars and spurs me to leap
to a safer and more noble realm.
And of your promises penned on paper in vain
And of your honor, I do reason and weep.

. . .

O return me to the time when loose and mild
to my blind ardor were bridle, bit, and rein.
O restore that face, angelical, serene again
and all the virtues buried with it, earth-defiled.

And all my erstwhile pacing, worrisome and wild
Now so heavy-slow in one near death's domain,
Return to me the water and the fire which my breast did
    contain
If you would satiate yourself with me once more, and be
    beguiled.

And if, Love, you only can survive
on bitter-sweet plaints of mortal men, you will expire:
From a tired old man, poor nourishment you will derive

For my soul will soon arrive at other shores
And there by arrows more compassionate, be shielded from
    yours;
Since burnt wood offers futile fuel to the fire.

If always one end alone is He who by His power
moves everything, high and wide;
nor does He reveal to us merely a single side
but more or less according as His graces shower.

To me in one way and to others everywhere
more or less clear, more luminously terse
according to the infirmity which does disperse
the intellect from proofs of its divine Mover.

And to the heart, most disposed, the more prehensile will
    cling,
so to say, His Face and His Force
and of that alone make a guide and lantern.

. . .

. . .

And find what conforms to his inmost part, and there turn.

O make me see thee in every place!
If I feel myself burning for mortal beauty
Nigh yours, mine will a spent fire be
And in yours I will be, as I have been, ablaze.

Dear my Lord, thee alone I call upon, invoke, praise
against my blind vain torment and misery.
Thou alone can, within and without, renew in me
My will, my sense, my small tardy worth and ways.

This divine soul for a while to Time you did give
And within this fleshy mold, frail and weary
You imprisoned it with a savage destiny.

What more can I do that thus I do not live?
Without thee, Lord, all good is lacking me and late,
Divinity alone can change our fate.

[224]

From the highest mountains, and from a great ruin
Hidden and surrounded by a great stone
I descended to find myself alone
in this low place, unwillingly, in such a tiny tomb.

When the sun was born, as Heaven decreed . . .

. . .

[225]

Whatever beautiful object I see
Passes to my heart at once through my eyes
upon so wide a way, of such capacity
it is open to a thousand, no less a hundred, of every size,

of every age, every sex; and I, in surprise
am afraid, weighed down by weariness, even more by jealousy
Nor among such varied faces can I surmise
Who, before my death, will bring me full felicity.

For if mortal beauty completely quenches passion,
then it did not descend together with the soul from heaven
Human is it then: a human hunger utterly.

But if it pass beyond, O Love, it scorns your name and is free
to seek another love, no longer fearful of this hide,
this base body lodging alongside.

Sonnet to Giorgio Vasari

(after the publication of his *Lives* . . . 1550)*

If with design and color you parallel
Nature; rather, by your style and art
Surpass her splendor, diminish her in part
by returning her to us more beautiful.

Then with learnèd hand, to the joy of your brothers,
You set upon a more worthy task: to write,
augmenting your fame, reducing hers; to indite
what still was lacking you, by lending life to others.

So that if throughout the centuries
others have rivalled her in beautiful creations;
They also yield; all must at its destined end arrive.

But now you set ablaze extinguished memories
Bringing them back—and yourself—against all
        expectations,
despite her, eternally alive.

* See Note 226

[227]

Those who don't want leaves
Let them not come here in May.⋆

⋆ Girardi suggests an analogy with Shakespeare's "Ripeness is all." Tusiani
reads it as "Everything at the right time." But typical of Michelangelo is that
he should express the admonition as a sequence of negatives. According to
Michelangelo the Younger, the motto hung over a door in the master's
house.

To what am I spurred by a lovely face's power?
Nothing else so delights me in this world.
To ascend alive among the blessèd spirits whirled,
Such grace, it seems, pales every other.

If the work with its maker is in harmony
What guilt would justice apportion to my days?
If I love, no, burn, honor and praise
Every noble soul expressive of divinity?

the unquiet soul, confused, does not find
in itself any other cause than some grave sin,
ill-recognized and yet not concealed within
from the immense Pity for each miserable mind.

I speak to thee, Lord, for all my efforts are blind
without your blood, and will not make a man blessed.
Have mercy upon me since I am born distressed
According to your law; nothing new has been designed.

Even in cold ice, the fire used to burn.
Now to me, cold ice is ardent fire in turn.
Loosened is the knot, Love, insoluble;
Now Death inhabits me where once was riot and revel.

That first love which gave it time and place,
in my extreme misery is a grave obstacle
to the weary soul . . .

With so much servitude, so much tedium,
Such false concepts, such great peril
to my soul—Here am I sculpting divine things.*

* This fragment of three hendecasyllables was written possibly while Miche-
langelo was working on the Nicodemus Pietà, intended for his own tomb.

. . .

Our fresh green age, my dear Lord, cannot comprehend
How much our tastes, loves, thoughts, desires
Change at the ultimate step when all will end.

The more it loses the world, the more the soul acquires,
Art and death do not go well together.
What more should I expect from my spent fires?

If in your name, some image I conceive,
Not without its peer, Death, does it come,
Whence art and genius are all undone.

But if as some assert, and I too believe,
that we shall live again, if destiny allow
then I will serve you should my art also follow.

Arrived at last is the course of my life
Through stormy seas, as in a fragile barque I toss
to the common port which all must cross
To render up accounts of good and evil.

Whence now I know how fraught with error still
Was the fond imagination which made of art
My idol and my monarch, and how vain that
Which every man despite himself desires.

Those amorous thoughts, once joyous, those frivolous fires,
What now? If toward a double death I draw?
One certain, I know, the other menacing me?

Painting nor sculpturing no more will allay
The soul turned toward that divine love at last
Which opened to us its arms upon the Cross.

[235]

My thoughts so endless, so full of folly have been
Now in the last years of my life, I should hone
them, restrict them to one thought alone
Guiding me to everlasting days serene.

But what can I do, Lord, if you do not come to me
with your familiar ineffable courtesy?

[236]

From day to day, from my earliest years,
Lord, you have been help to me and guide to me
Whence my soul still sets its faith in Thee
in your double help for my double grief and tears.

the fables of the world have from me taken
the time allotted us to contemplate God.
And not only have his blessings been forgot,
But with them, more than without, into sin I've fallen.

That which makes others wise, makes me blind, befallen,
foolish, slow to recognize my error
lacking hope, yet ever grows my desire
that freed by Thee, from self-love I'll awaken.

Dear my Lord, the road that mounts to Heaven,
O cut in half for me! — that half even
I cannot climb unless Your Hand you proffer.

Cause me to hate all that the world values
And all the fair things I esteem and choose
So that before death, eternal life I savor.

No baser thing, more vile, terrestrial
than I, without Thee, as I am and feel;
Hence to my lofty longing I make appeal
and pardon beg for my weakness and weary will.

Therefore enchain me, Lord, with that celestial chain
which links to itself every gift of paradise.
Of faith I speak, toward which I spur myself and agonize
And yet entire grace—my guilt—I do not attain.

So much the greater for me; the more rare
that gift of gifts, and greater yet since it's not here,
For in itself the world has no peace or content.

And since of your blood you were not miserly,
By such a gift of clemency, what was meant
if heaven opens not to us by any other key?

Relieved of this heavy corpse, this importunate alarm
Dear my Lord, and freed from the world
Like a frail ship wearily I turn to Thee, hurled
from a frightful storm to sweet calm.

The thorns, the nails, this and th' other palm
and your benign humble pitying face
promise, for so much repentance, grace
and to the sad soul, salvation and balm.

Let not your holy eyes in judgment gaze
at my past. Heedless be your chaste ear,
Nor point out my transgressions with your arm severe.

Let your blood alone wash and glaze
and touch my faults. Let full pardon enfold
me, abounding all the more, the more I grow old.

Well do I think and know some guilt lives
hidden in me, oppressing my soul. And in that fire,
in martyrdom, the fury of the senses deprives
my heart of peace; and hope deserts desire.

But who is with you, Love? What do you fear
might sully grace before its departure?

. . .

Sweet would be my prayers to you, if you would lend
me strength to pray. For in my fragile fields
there is no plot which good fruit yields
born of itself, which You do not send.

You alone are the seed of works chaste and pious
Which blossom there where you are the sower.
No one can follow you by his own power
If you show not your sacred ways to us.

[242]

Laden with the years and full of sin
with all my evil ways deep-rooted beneath,
I see myself nearing the double death
And yet I nourish still my heart with poison.

Nor sufficient strength do I possess within
to change my life, love, customs, destiny
without the convoy of your luminous divinity;
curbing fallacious courses, guide and rein.

Dear my Lord, it's not enough that you implore
me to aspire to heaven alone so that my soul might be
Not created out of nothing as before.

But rather that you strip and purge it of mortality
I pray you cut in half the steep way remaining
And more clear and certain make my returning.

[243]

Even when I grieve and groan, still to me dear
is every thought whereby memory re-awakens
Time past; and reason questions me and reckons
of days lost, beyond refuge and repair.

Dear to me only because when death is near
I learn thus how evanescent and mistaken
is human pleasure, and how sad that grace does not beckon
in one's final years. And mercy for one's sins is rare.

For although one may await your promise,
To hope, O Lord, is perhaps too presumptuous
that love forgive all excessive tardiness.

But yet it seems that by your blood we comprehend
that if your martyrdom seems not to have been for us
Yet measureless your precious gifts will never end.

Certain of death but not yet of the hour
Life is brief and leaves little to me;
Pleasing to the senses but not the proper bower
for the soul which begs me only that I die.

The world is blind and evil still holds power
to conquer and submerge all the best behavior.
Spent is the light and with it all valor.
Falsity triumphs and Truth does not flower.

When O Lord will come to be what the faithful
still await? For too much delay
truncates hope, and makes the soul mortal.

What is it worth to promise supernal day
If Death arrive first? without refuge, without fail,
Fixing us forever in that state he did assail?

Often it happens great yearning will promise
my abundant years many years more,
Not that death ever ceases to draw near the door;
And where he brings less grief, he hastens less.

Why await more life to enjoy and caress
if only in misery is God adored?
Good luck and long survival do not accord
But harm us more, the more they seem to bless.

And if at times my heart's assailed by your grace and birth
Dear my Lord, that ardent zeal so near it
which comforts and reassures my spirit.

Since my own worth is nothing worth
That would be the very moment to ascend,
for the more the time, the sooner good resolutions end.

If a long span of wretched foolish inclinations
Requires more time to purge it to its contrariety
Death, already close, will not concede it to me
Nor curb my evil ways from old wants to new directions.

[247]

The blessèd spirits were no less happy than disturbed
and aggrieved that you, not they, should suffer death;
Whence the closed doors of heaven and earth
Were flung open to man by your blood.

Happy that you redeemed what you did create,
Assuming the primal error of his miserable fate;
Aggrieved, that by your suffering and bitter pain
on the Cross, servant of servants you became.

Of who you were, and whence, heaven did proclaim
by signs: darkening its eyes, the earth opening again
Making the mountains tremble, and the turbid waters overwhelm.

Freeing the great Fathers from the tenebrous realm
And the ugly angels submerged to graver grief, forlorn
And only Man rejoiced, baptised, re-born.

[248]

By the sugar, the mule, and the candles
(to which you add a flask of Malvasio)
Outweighed is all my fortune so,
that the scales I'm returning to Saint Michael.

Too much fair weather collapses the sails
of my fragile bark on a windless sea
So that it loses its way and seems to be
a wisp of straw the cruel ocean assails.

With all respect and gratitude for the gifts you bring:
this food, and drink, and the mule for frequent motion
So dear and kind to all my needs is your devotion,

Dear my lord, I would still be nothing
to give you all I am in merit of what you sent
For paying a debt is not giving a present.

[249]

By the Cross and by grace and manifold misery
I am certain we will meet in Heaven, Monsignor.*
But even before that ultimate gasp, even before,
to take pleasure on earth seems good to me.

Even if the rough road through mountains and through seas
Keeps us far apart, yet spirit and zeal
care not for obstacles, nor snow nor ice we feel,
Nor can the wings of thought be chained or locked by keys.

Hence in my thoughts I am always with you,
weeping and speaking of my dead Urbino**
Were he alive, we would be there perhaps together

As already I am in fantasy. His death, alas,
draws me in haste to another road and pass
where he awaits me to dwell with him forever.

* This sonnet was written in reply to one sent to Michelangelo by the Arch-
  bishop Beccadelli, from Ragusa, Dalmatia, in February 1556.
** The artist's beloved servant who died 2 December 1555 after twenty-six
  years of devoted service.

More and more things bring sadness to my eyes
and to my heart—as many as the world contains
What would I do with life, were it not sustained
by the gift of yourself, dearest of courtesies?

For my dismal habits and wretched instances
Amidst the thick shadows where I remain,
Help I hope to find, as well as pardon for my shame.
For revealing yourself to us, you owe such promises.

By no other means do you strip me of love,
and all those passions perilous and vain
than those which adverse fortune and strange instances contain,
And thus your friends from this world you remove.

Dear my Lord, you alone vest and divest us,
And by your blood purify the soul—by such purgations—
of its infinite guilts and human perturbations

. . .

Notes

1. Beginning of a sonnet dated by Girardi 1503 when Michelangelo was twenty-eight years old. Written on the back of a page bearing the drawing of an apostle and a battle scene. Alongside the verses, sketches of capitals and a mask.

2. 1503-04. On a sheet with sketches of a leg and other subjects.

3. Sonnet written alongside the drawings of horses and a battle scene. After 1504.

4. Written on the back of a letter from Michelangelo's brother, 24 December 1507, sent to the artist in Bologna where he was then working on the statue of Pope Julius II. The verses seem to have been inspired by love for a young Bolognese girl. On the same page a verse:

> She burns me and binds me and clasps me
> and seems a chunk of sugar.

5. Giovanni da Pistoia was a literatus, a functionary in the Medici duchy, and later in 1540, Chancellor of the Florentine Academy. We know of five sonnets by Giovanni addressed to Michelangelo.

6. The Dante-derived invective against Pistoia (a town thirty miles from Florence) seems to place this poem, also a caudal sonnet, with the preceding. Perhaps it was addressed to the same friend.

7. Addressed to Pope Julius II (1503-1513), whose personality like the artist's was characterized by *terribilità*, and with whom Michelangelo frequently quarreled.

8. Michelangelo the Younger thought this was sent to Giovanni da Pistoia, but the tone seems to me less burlesque than bitter. The poet was actually referring to Rome under the bellicose Julius II, especially during the years of the Holy League and the battle of Ravenna (1512) when the Pope was more often on the battlefield wearing armor under his papal robes, than in the Vatican. That Michelangelo felt he was in "Turkey" is his ironic comment on the unChristian character of Italy at that time.

13. This madrigal was set to music by Bartolomeo Tromboncino, the famous Italian composer who spent most of his life in the service of the Marchese of Mantova. The setting was published in a book of his songs, in Naples in 1518, the first of the very few Michelangelo poems published during his lifetime.

14. From a drawing of two sepulchres for the Medici Tombs on which Michelangelo worked from 1520/21 on.

15. Also relating to the Medici Tombs.

16. Madrigal on the back of a sketch of details of sepulchres for the Medici Tombs.

17. A distich from the same sheet as the preceding.

18. Scribbled on the back of a letter from Stefano di Tommaso in Florence 20 April 1521 to Michelangelo in Carrara where he was then selecting marble blocks for the Medici Tombs. The poor handwriting may explain why so many editors (and consequently translators) have interpreted *verno* (winter) as *primavera* (spring).

19. A group of hendecasyllables written on the back of a letter from Giovanni da Udine to Michelangelo in Florence, dated 8th of Easter 1522.

20. Incomplete madrigal written on the same sheet with household expenses, a date 25 November 1522 and architectural sketches in pen and pencil probably relating to the New Sacristy in San Lorenzo.

21. Three burlesque octaves from a pen drawing of a mother and child standing. Some editors interpret this as a Madonna and Christ Child. On the same sheet architectural sketches probably by Michelangelo's assistant Antonio Mini, relating to the walls of the Medici Chapel, which would date the poem in the 1520's.

23. Verses written on a sheet with the beginning of a letter from Michelangelo to Giovan Francesco Fattucci, chaplain of the cathedral, S. Maria del Fiore in Florence, dated January 1524. This is the "hard evidence" which induces Girardi to place the poem in Michelangelo's middle years. Frey, on the other hand (followed by numerous Italian and American editors and translators) considers these verses as the sad meditations of a man nearing his eightieth year. I follow Girardi: Michelangelo was capable of old-age meditations at all stages of his life.

24. This sonnet and the two succeeding (one incomplete and one caudal) are all found on the same sheet. Frey dates them toward 1550 (Michelangelo's seventy-fifth year); Girardi twenty-five years earlier.

28. Incomplete sonnet written in graphite on the back of a page containing architectural designs and a sketch for one of the Medici Tombs.

32. Fragment of a sonnet written on the back of a letter from 'Sandro iscarpellino (marble-cutter) in Charara' (Carrara) dated 8 October 1525.

33. Incomplete sestina. On the back of a drawing of a Virgin and Child. The autograph, scratched out, is almost illegible and has been reconstructed by Girardi.

39. Fragment of a sonnet. Back of the sheet a sketch, probably by a student, of Christ rising from the tomb.

45. Capitolo in tercets, incomplete. On the page "a pen sketch of a hand with the index finger turned toward the writing." (Girardi). Frey attributes the capitolo to the period of poems written for the death of Vittoria Colonna (25 February 1547); Girardi rejects this,

primarily on the basis of the handwriting and dates the poem about 1528 or soon after.

46. On the manuscript under the poem Michelangelo continues the thought in prose:

LIONARDO

She was alone in this world in exalting virtues with her own great virtue; she had no one to draw the bellows. Now in heaven she will have many companions since only those who loved the virtues dwell there. I hope therefore that from above she will perfect my own hammer here below. At least now in heaven she will have someone to handle the bellows; for here on earth she had no companion at the forge where virtues are exalted.

Scholars differ with regard to the person for whom this sonnet was intended. Frey believes it was written after the death of Vittoria Colonna; Girardi considers it rather after the death of a friend of Michelangelo, or after his brother Buonarroto's death in 1528. Buonarroto left a nine-year-old son named Lionardo who might have been the object of the prose meditation above.

Girardi recalls that the image of Hammer and Divine Smith are clearly derived from Dante's Paradiso (11, 127–32).

47. Frey believed this poem was written after the death of Vittoria Colonna; the reference to *carte* ('pages') on which poems were written would seem to confirm his supposition.

Girardi however, denies Vittoria Colonna as the dedicatee, and considers that the poem might have been inspired by the death of Michelangelo's brother (1528), or that of Febo di Poggio, drawing attention to line 6: ". . . Sun of the Sun." In Italian the name Febo = Phoebus = Sun! But ". . . *sol del sol*" serves very well indeed as an exaltation of Vittoria Colonna. As for the masculine endings, these might well relate to *ministro*, 'minister', not necessarily a man.

On the same page there are various sketches, among which a bearded old man in profile, staring at a woman with nude pendulent breasts. Frey considered the image of the woman as referring to Vittoria Colonna, and the old man as Michelangelo himself. I doubt very much that Michelangelo would ever conceive of such an image for his Platonically beloved. As in so many cases, drawings and verses do not necessarily relate to the same period or theme.

49. Quartino on the back of a page where is written by another hand a prayer to the Eternal Father invoking liberation of the city from plague.

Girardi speculates that the verses probably were written during the Siege of Florence (1530) or shortly after. Obviously the lines have nothing to do with siege or plague. Michelangelo, thrifty as a Tuscan peasant, used any paper at hand for his poetic musings.

51. On a page with red chalk drawings relating to the Medici Tombs.

52. Fragment of a sonnet behind a note from Figiovanni advising Michelangelo of the desire expressed by the Marchese del Vasto and the Archbishop of Capua to see a Michelangelo 'cartone' (big drawing) of the Magdalen.

54. These thirteen stanzas are obviously influenced by the burlesque style of Berni. On one of the pages an expense account written about 1531.

56. On the back of a letter from Sebastiano del Piombo to Michelangelo, dated 8 June 1532.

58. An angry reproval of those who question the chaste nature of Michelangelo's love-friendship, and an equally angry reproval of the belovèd friend for his lending credence to these accusations.

Girardi speculates that the sonnet was probably written to Cavalieri during the early days of their friendship, 1532-33.

59. This sonnet and the two succeeding, all relating to Cavalieri, are written on a letter from the painter Giuliano Buggiardini in Florence to Michelangelo in Rome 5 August 1532.

62. The imagery of this quattrain is very similar to No's 191 and 192 of the del Riccio collection.

63. This fragment of a sonnet is behind a rough of an undated letter from Michelangelo to Andrea Quaratesi.

64. Sonnet found within a letter from Figiovanni to Michelangelo in Rome, 23 November 1532.

65. These stanzas celebrating the simple healthy lives of shepherds seem to have been inspired by Michelangelo's sojourn in Spoleto in 1556 when he fled Rome in fear of an imminent invasion by the Duke of Alba. Frey therefore dates these verses after 1556.

Girardi, however, places the verses much earlier (1536) on the basis among other things of the handwriting.

Whatever the dating, this bucolic and rustic idealization is rare in Michelangelo's *oeuvre* whether in painting or poetry. Like most Florentines, then and now, the artist liked to consider himself a *campagnolo* (a countryman) at heart while he remained resolutely as much as possible in the city.

By the ninth stanza, this celebration of simple rustic virtue slants off into an allegory that will remind English readers of Spencer's *Fairy Queen*.

66. Six allegorical verses which seem related to the preceding in praise of the rustic life. The Allegories have been variously interpreted: Michelangelo the Younger thought that the Giant signified Fury, the woman alongside him Pride and the seven children the seven deadly sins.

68. The manuscript of this sestina is very difficult to decipher. Frey only published the first two lines. The complete sestina is a reconstruction by Girardi.

72. Although some scholars consider this written for Cavalieri, it is noteworthy that (like No. 122 of the del Riccio collection) some of the preparatory variants were directed to a woman: a reversal of Michelangelo's usual sexual transmogrifications.

73. Written on the fragment of a letter to Sebastiano del Piombo.

74. Frey speculates that this sonnet was inspired by a loved woman after the death of Vittoria Colonna. Girardi rejects this in favor of Cavalieri as addressee.

75. Girardi is convinced this poem is dedicated to Cavalieri during the summer of 1533 when the artist sent the young nobleman several drawings of mythological subjects which Vittoria Colonna (whom other scholars assign as dedicatee) would certainly have considered: '*turpissime pitture*', 'disgraceful pictures.'

76. Probably for Cavalieri. The poem contains certain affinities of expression found in a letter from Michelangelo to Cavalieri, 1 January 1533.

77. Frey considered this for Cavalieri.

78. Sonnet for Cavalieri, among the most explicit and important.

81. This deeply moving capitolo was written after the death of Michelangelo's father, Lodovico, in Florence, 1534, at the age of almost ninety (stanza 14, line 1: "Ninety times has the sun . . ."). Michelangelo was present at the funeral and paid all the expenses. He departed for Rome shortly after, never to return to his native city.

82. This sonnet which will remind the English reader of John Dunne's metaphysical poetry, has been collocated by Frey with the late religious poetry. Girardi, however, on the basis of the handwriting, places it in the earlier period when Michelangelo was writing poetry to Cavalieri. The erotic-religious ambiguity suggests either dating.

The coexistence of contrarieties, brilliantly stated in the first quatrain, is central to Michelangelo's psychology. Intellect, or even the works prescribed by the Church, cannot resolve his dilemma. Only the light of grace can save him, grace predestined (*preditto lume*), beyond his will. All this seems pretty close to the Lutheran Reformists until the appeal in the final tercet that grace be sent not only to the individual sinner but to the 'beautiful bride' (*bella sposa*), the Roman Catholic Church, which is surely not a Protestant notion.

The tension and tightness of all this is typical of Michelangelo's poetry — and of his theologizing.

83. The masochistic and macabre imagery reminds us of the flayed skin of Saint Bartholomew in the Sistine Chapel. Written on the back of a letter from Pierantonio, a friend of the Cardinal Ridolfi, to Michelangelo in Rome, undated, but probably in the Spring of 1535.

84. Some scholars believe these tercets were written for an unknown woman: Girardi believes for Cavalieri.

85. Benedetto Varchi in his famous lecture on a poem of Miche-

langelo at the Florence Academy, *had* this to say of its inspirer: "/The sonnet was/ . . . addressed to M. Tommaso Cavalieri, a young Roman nobleman in whom I found, when I knew him in Rome, such charming manners (other than his incomparable physical beauty) and such excellent talent and gracious behavior that he well deserved, and still deserves to be all the more loved the more he is known."

"Knight' in the last line is the exact meaning (in the singular) of Tommaso's surname Cavalieri.

86. Sonnet which some scholars believe inspired by the death of Febo di Poggio, or the rupture between Michelangelo and the young Roman. This attribution is based upon the seemingly explicit allusions to the name *Febo* (Phoebus, Sun) and *Poggio* (hill). Notwithstanding this, numerous commentators have indicated Vittoria Colonna as the inspirer of these verses, or thought of a political interpretation whereby Phoebus would stand for the City of Florence.

87. Incomplete sonnet, also seemingly addressed to Febo di Poggio.

88. This is the first of four sonnets on the theme of Night. Girardi groups them all together (G 101, 102, 103, 104); Frey, however, although he assigns them all to the period of the Last Judgment, publishes them disparately: two in the del Riccio collection, and two at this point in the chronology. I follow Frey on the assumption that Michelangelo selected only two Night poems for his intended publication. I wish to keep the del Riccio collection intact as a clue to Michelangelo's judgment on his own poetry. The omission of these two great sonnets, however, from those selected for publication suggests that criteria, other than quality, influenced the selection.

The other two sonnets on this nocturnal theme are numbered here 131 and 132.

89. One of Michelangelo's most famous sonnets. See previous note.

92. Madrigal which Frey (as well as Girardi) assigns to the first poetry written for Vittoria Colonna.

93. Girardi believes this was destined for Vittoria Colonna or some unknown woman. I should say the overwrought mannerist imagery definitely rules out the austere Marchese as either inspiration or dedication.

On the back of the manuscript there is an amusing petulant letter to the artist's nephew, admonishing the boy to learn how to write better 'in order to become somebody'. In one of the drafts of this note Michelangelo even imitates the crude uncertain hand of children who do not know yet how to hold a pen properly.

94. The first quatrain of this magnificent sonnet intended for Vittoria Colonna epitomizes Michelangelo's aesthetics and his method of work in sculpture. The Platonic notion that the Idea preexists its material realization becomes the notion that the statue preexists in

the "excess" of the marble block; the sculptor removed this excess to reveal the finished work—a process of dis-covery or uncovering to reveal the work which has been initially created by the Prime Sculptor. But this process of discovery requires navigation, the trained mind, the hand that obeys the intellect.

Puzzling is the fact that this great poem, undoubtedly written before 1546, was not chosen by the author or his friend del Riccio for their projected publication.

95. Madrigal related to the preceding.

96. For Vittoria Colonna.

97. For Vittoria Colonna.

98. This madrigal of two sestine for Vittoria Colonna was composed, according to Frey, when the Marchese was living in the Convent of Santa Caterina di Viterbo.

Again we find Michelangelo's assertion of Beauty as equivalent to Divine Truth (*lucerna* e *specchio*), centuries before John Keats' celebrated equation:

> "Beauty is truth, truth beauty,"—that is all
> ye know on earth, and all ye need to know.

But Michelangelo's Beauty is contrasted clearly and severely to sense which of course inculcated another contradiction since he was so vulnerable to sensory perception and experience. The grip of this contradiction can only be sundered by grace, a notion close to that of the contemporary Reformation.

100. Petrarchesque in imagery and spirit, this madrigal for the "Lady fair and cruel" was not included by Frey for the del Riccio collection. I agree with Girardi that it was probably intended for publication.

102. A curiously and unnecessarily intricate madrigal, probably dedicated to Vittoria Colonna.

103. In the letter to Fattucci which accompanied this madrigal and the following sonnet: ". . .I send you some of my new things (*novelle*) that I wrote for the Marchesa of Pescara, who loved me greatly as I no less did love her. Death has taken away from me a great friend."

Possibly intended for the del Riccio collection although it is not so included by Frey.

104. Michelangelo the Younger speculates that this sonnet for Vittoria Colonna accompanied a self-portrait the artist had given the Marchesa.

110. This sonnet has been referred by various editors to the 'cruel fair lady,' to Luigi del Riccio, even to Vittoria Colonna! (by Michelangelo the Younger).

The evidence is overwhelming, however, that it refers to del Riccio who was at that time helping the artist prepare a collection of his poems for publication; and on two occasions when Michelangelo had been gravely ill (1544 and again 1546), taken the artist into the Strozzi Palace in Rome and tenderly cared for him.

A letter from Michelangelo to del Riccio, while acknowledging gratitude to the friend who had "saved me from death", bitterly reproves del Riccio for not having respected his wishes, for having made a 'shop' (*bottega*) of his work; and pleads with him to destroy "that print" (*quella stampa*) and to burn those which are already printed. The words *stampa* and *stampate* are ambiguous as they may refer either to an engraving or verses published without Michelangelo's knowledge.

110A. Thematically this madrigal would seem to relate to the preceding bitter sonnet. Further confirmation is provided by Luigi's response in this poem:

> No courtesy / should be harmful / between friends, and the traditional (*antica*) opinion / of the world has been this: / that everything should be / shared (*commune*) between them: even to go to prison / and die for each other: and rightfully / possessions, life and honor they give each other. / Hence no question can arise between us / since there is nothing friendship does not forgive.

All the more perplexing therefore is Frey's inclusion of Michelangelo's poem in the projected publication whose chief sponsor was *del Riccio*! For this reason I have removed it from the collection and placed it here instead.

112. There are two readings of this sonnet revolving on the presence or absence of a comma, and the inclinations of the commentator. Guasti and Frey believed the sonnet was written for Vittoria Colonna and therefore the word "donna" (line 2 of the first tercet) is a vocative (as I have rendered it).

Girardi on the other hand believes the sonnet was intended for Cavalieri and reads (line 2 of the first tercet): "Woman is too dissimilar . . ." a plea against love of women, indeed equating physical love as exclusively love of women. Grammatically this argument is dubious since the verse *donna è dissimil troppo* is impossible; in Italian nouns used in a general sense require the definite article, in this case *la* donna, as in *la donna è mobile*, "Women are inconstant."

Apart from this grammatical underbrush, the sonnet is clearly an affirmation of the superiority of spiritual over *all* sensual love, whether male or female. This exaltation of the Platonic ladder of love is a familiar Renaissance theme, ecstatically put forth by Bembo in Castiglione's *Cortegiano*, and pictorially in Titian's *Sacred and Profane Love*.

117. Some scholars argue from the variants that this madrigal was originally intended for Febo di Poggio; others find Petrarchian reminiscences. At any rate, the final version prepared for publication was almost certainly addressed to Vittoria Colonna.

118. For the *donna bella e crudele* ('the beautiful cruel Lady')

119. This is the fourth version of a concept Michelangelo had been grappling with since 1524. The first three versions seem to be addressed to a woman; the final version, intended for the publication, is addressed to Febo di Poggio, according to Girardi. Other editors consider this madrigal inspired by Vittoria Colonna, which seems absurd to me on the basis of the first line alone. I would assign it among those intended for the 'fair cruel lady'.

120. The consensus is that this belongs with those poems written during the sojourn of the Marchese Vittoria Colonna at Viterbo. (c. 1541–45)

121. For the 'beautiful cruel lady.'

122. There are numerous versions of this madrigal. From the variants it appears that the poem was originally directed to a woman, then utilized for Cavalieri. To judge by the poems, Michelangelo was quite fluid in his choice of erotic objects.

126. For the 'donna bella e crudele'. See line 12: "O my savage wild star!"

127. Also for the 'beautiful cruel lady'.

128. This is the famous epigram written in response to the one by Giovanni Strozzi (1545) in praise of Michelangelo's allegorical figure of Night in the Medici Chapel.

129. For Cavalieri. On a page with architectural drawings.

130. Also for Cavalieri.

131. This and the following are the third and fourth of the sonnets dedicated to Night. Girardi groups them al together on the basis of theme and their likely destination who seems to have been Cavalieri. I follow Frey in collocating this and the following in the del Riccio Collection. The first two in this book are numbered 88 and 89.

132. Idem above.

133. For the 'fair cruel lady'.

134. The last line of this madrigal, probably for Vittoria Colonna, reminds one of the last line of the youthful sonnet to the Bolognese girl: (No 4)

What then is left for my poor arms to do?

135-136-137-138. All inspired by and addressed to the 'fair cruel lady'. 138 picks up the Night theme again but in a different context.

139-140. On the manuscript bearing this madrigal and the following, Michelangelo wrote to del Riccio:

Messer Luigi, you who possess the spirit of poetry, I beg you to trim and put in order whichever of these madrigals seem less unworthy because I have to give it to our friend. Your Michel
. . .

Girardi surmises the friend might have been Cavalieri. I doubt it; the gift which Cavalieri offered in exchange was friendship which did not cost "the price that one must pay".

141. This madrigal exists in three versions: two from the mid 1530's, the third reworked for the del Riccio Collection (1546). I find it difficult to accept Girardi's speculation that the poem was inspired by Cavalieri. Surely ten years after their first encounters, Michelangelo had accepted the young Roman's much cooler, Platonic definition of their friendship which was to last until the artist's death in 1564.

142. The autograph includes a brief postscript by Michelangelo to Donato Giannotti:

To Messer Donato, please patch up these badly-made things.

146. On the manuscript: "To messer Donato Giannotti, his Michelagniolo."

147-148. The two sonnets to Dante. Although Frey includes both in the del Riccio Collection, inexplicably he does not group them together.

Michelangelo was highly reputed in his own day as a Danteist and in 1546 he appears in Donato Giannotti's *I Dialoghi dei giorni che Dante consumò nel cercare l'Inferno e il Purgatorio.* 'Dialogues on the number of days Dante spent in traversing Hell and Purgatory.'

Apparently the poet considered the second sonnet less inspired than the first, for on the autograph there is a letter to Giannotti: "Messer Donato, you ask of me that which I don't possess."

149. On the manuscript "To Messer Luigi del Riccio dearest friend in the Banchi" (a section of Rome wherein resided most of the Florentines), "Your Michelagniolo Buonarroti" with a variant of the two final lines and note: "Take this worthless deficiency (*manco tristo*) for Messer Donato's judgment."

151. Madrigal probably for Cavalieri. The manuscript bears several lines directed

To messer Luigi del Riccio in Banchi—

Messer Luigi, my dear lord. Arcadente's song is considered very beautiful, and since according to what he says, intended to give me no less pleasure than you who commissioned it, I don't want to be ungrateful to him in such a matter. Therefore I beg you to think of some present to give him, either silks or money, and let me know and I'll do as you say without question. That's all I have to tell you. I commend myself to you and to Messer Donato and to heaven and earth.

Your Michelagniolo once again.

"Arcadente" is Jacob Arcadelt (1505-1568), the Franco-Flemish composer who had served the Medici in Florence from 1540-51, then went in San Marco in Venice, and from 1540-51 was in papal service as master of the Sistine Choir. Michelangelo felt honored that the famous composer should have set several of his poems to music and included them in Arcadelt's first book of madrigals, *Il primo Libro de' Madrigali d' Arcadelt* published in 1543.

152. Madrigal for the 'Lady fair and cruel'. Both parts were set to music separately by Arcadelt (see above), and published by Guasti as two separate poems. Frey as well as Girardi considers it a single poem in two parts.

Girardi interprets the work as Love's response to the questions put by the poet in the first part. Guasti discerns instead, in the second part, a political allusion (the woman would be the city of Florence).

155. Another example of ambiguity: planned or the result of endless tacking between confession and concealment. Girardi thinks this madrigal is addressed to the 'cruel fair lady' rather than for Vittoria Colonna, as Frey had supposed.

157. Sonnet for the 'donna bella e crudele'. An earlier version was addressed to a man, perhaps Cavalieri and then reworked in the feminine, a procedure Michelangelo also followed in his studies for the Libyan Sibyl of the Sistine Vault.

159. Since this madrigal was selected for the del Riccio collection, eight years after the hated Duke Alessandro was slain, was Michelangelo now applying the allegory to the new ruler of Florence, Duke Cosimo I?

160. The madrigal, probably for Vittoria Colonna, bears the postscript to Riccio: "Since you want some verselets, I can't send you other than that which I have on hand. Your loss, and your Michelagniolo's best wishes."

162. Madrigal probably for the "lady fair and cruel." Under the poem Michelangelo wrote: "For sculptors".

167. This poem, like the five preceding, was written for the "donna". This madrigal bears a postscript for Riccio: "With thanks for the melons and the wine, I pay you with a *polizino* (a little doggerel)." Frey deduces from this that the madrigal dates from 1544 during the period when Michelangelo was writing the epitaphs for Cecchino Bracci. (see pp. 116-127)

168. Probably sent to del Riccio like the preceeding.

169. This too, addressed to the Donna crudele, must have been sent to del Riccio, for on the manuscript is written: "This for the *ravviggiuoli* (a kind of tender young beans); the other for the olives should it be worth that much."

170. The adjective "alta" instead of the frequent "altera" points to "lofty" rather than "proud" or "haughty", further evidence that the poem speaks of Vittoria Colonna.

This is the only poem that makes metaphoric use of sculptural casting. Michelangelo did not consider casting (from modeling) as true sculpture which was the art of 'taking away' (*levare*), i.e. carving. But here the imagery suits his poetic purposes.

173. Madrigal of uncertain destination. On the autograph is written: "For last night's duck," probably for Luigi del Riccio.

177. For the "fair cruel lady". On the manuscript a postscript from Michelangelo to Riccio: "This is truly a scribble; all my regards to you."

179. A note to Riccio is on the autograph: "Messer Luigi, Please send me the last madrigal, which you don't understand, so that I may fix it up because that scribble-gatherer (*sollecitore de' polizini*) who is Urbino was in such a hurry that he didn't let me look it over. About getting together tomorrow you must excuse me because the weather is bad and I have things to do at home. Later we can do the same thing that we would do tomorrow, this Lent at Lunghezza with a big keg."

In his letters to Riccio Michelangelo often called "polizini" (literally, pawn tickets) — squibs, scribblings — the pages on which he recopied his verses. Urbino was his servant and La Lunghezza was a farm (tenuta) formerly belonging to the Medici House, near Rome. Guasti thought this poem was written after the death of Cecchino Bracci. Girardi assigns it instead to the "cruel fair lady," or more precisely, among the poems of that period.

180. Madrigal for Vittoria Colonna. On the sheet is written in Michelangelo's hand: "A rachonciar di dì." "To be fixed up by day."

181. Unquestionably for the "cruel" — in this case, "savage" — beautiful lady. On the manuscript: "This one I don't set down as the usual scribble but because of a dream I had."

182. On the manuscript of this madrigal are two lines in chalk in Michelangelo's hand:

> Song born at night in the middle of the bed
> To be put to rights tomorrow evening.

And at the right on the back: "It would be sweet as Adam's apple, but I have no more apples in my body."

183. Frey considered this for Vittoria Colonna which I find most unlikely considering the outspoken nature of some of the imagery ... On the manuscript a postscript: "Old Love has put forth a branch or rather a thallus." If this relates to the poem, it would be an even stronger argument against Frey's attribution.

184. Madrigal possibly for the "donna . . ." On one of the manuscripts of the variants, in Michelangelo's hand to Riccio: "This is for the trout; the sonnet about which I spoke will be for the pepper, which is worth less, but I cannot write. My regards to you!"

188. Madrigal inspired by Vittoria Colonna. Alongside the manuscript is written: "It is not fitting to bestow a palace upon someone who wants only half a loaf of bread"; this notion, directed to del Riccio is expressed in the madrigal itself.

190. Sonnet probably for the "cruel fair lady." On the manuscript a postscript: "For one of the *buctagre*" (*bottarga*: a sort of mullet or tuna fish roe-cake).

193-94. Also for the "donna" . . . The autograph is written on blue-gray paper with a postscript: "Of divine things one speaks in an azure field."

206. There are numerous reworkings of this sonnet. On one of the pages, amidst the verses, may be discerned a pencil sketch of a plan for the facade of St. Peter's on which Michelangelo began to work in *1546*.

208. On the manuscript Michelangelo wrote: *Mandato*. 'Dispatched'. If the madrigal dates from after Vittoria Colonna's death (25 Feb. 1547), as it seems to, does *mandato* mean sent (or "dispatched") to del Riccio for the intended publication? Or is the word used metaphorically?

210. This sonnet is collocated by Frey to the period of the most fervid correspondence with Vittoria Colonna. It is also the final poem of the del Riccio Collection as Frey has reconstructed it. Girardi places it much earlier, perhaps by ten years, and deduces that it was intended for Cavalieri.

211. This madrigal of which numerous versions exist, is a tangled web of obscurities and obliquities. The dedication is not clear though some editors have opted unconvincingly for Vittoria Colonna.

212. On the autograph a pen drawing of a knee for the St. Lawrence of the Last Judgment. The handwriting would date the poem much later. Michelangelo, like a thrifty Tuscan farmer, grew many crops from the same soil: writing drafts of poems and letters over drawings which he had on hand. There are numerous variations, heavily re-worked.

214. This madrigal on the death of Vittoria Colonna (who died at the age of fifty-seven) is curious in its profusion of conceits of calling loans and redeeming debts.

215. Sonnet on the death of Vittoria Colonna.

216. This famous *capitolo* has come down to us in a single copy written in the hand of Donato Giannotti's copyist. Line 36:

And in a bowl three pills of pitch are.

was interpreted by Guasti to mean "I have three stones in my bladder." During the years 1548-49 Michelangelo suffered greatly from kidney stones.

218. Madrigal written over a pencil sketch relating to the Last Judgment which the artist completed in 1550 at the age of seventy-five.

223. This cannot possibly be other than a religious sonnet. Yet the "Dear my Lord" is puzzling. Usually addressed to Tommaso Cavalieri or some other terrestrial friend.

224. Frey places this fragment during the period when Michelangelo was working at St. Peter's from 1547 to 1550, during which time the artist found himself literally in a desert of stone.

225. A confession of Michelangelo's protean all-inclusive

capacity — indeed vulnerability, both in a qualitative and quantitative sense — for loving.

But all human passion is ultimately inadequate, and the artist passes beyond that to seek another love, transcendent to the *bassa spoglia* — the 'base body'.

226. Sonnet dedicated to Giorgio Vasari in gratitude for the gift of the first edition of *The Lives of the Most Excellent Painters Sculptors and Architects* published in March 1550; Michelangelo was the only living artist included. The sonnet has been handed down to us by Vasari himself who added it to his biography of Michelangelo:

> "That year Vasari had completed the publication of the *Lives of the Most Excellent Painter Sculptors and Architects*, in Florence; and he had not included the life of any living artist except that of Michelangelo although there were some other aged artists still alive. And thus he presented the work to Michelangelo who received it with great joy, since Vasari had recorded in it many things about him as the dean and most judicious of artists. And no sooner had he read it than Michelangelo sent him the present sonnet which, in memory of his love, it pleases me to place here."

234. This famous sonnet was sent to Vasari with this note (19 September 1554):
"You too will perhaps say I am an old fool for still wanting to write sonnets, but since many people accuse me of senility, it is my duty to write." Michelangelo was then seventy-nine years old.

Vasari replied with a sonnet composed according to the same rhyme-scheme, together with a letter (lost) exhorting him, in the name of Duke Cosimo de' Medici, to return to Florence.

236. 'Double grief' relates probably to the 'double death' so often mentioned by Michelangelo in his old age: that is, death of the body and death of the soul.

Frey's speculation that the *doppi affanni* of the last line relate to the deaths of Michelangelo's father and brother would date the fragment twenty years earlier.

237. Sonnet sent to Monsignore Ludovico Beccadelli formerly apostolic nunzio in Vienna, who had been named Archbishop of Ragusa and was preparing to depart for that city. Beccadelli replied to Michelangelo with a sonnet structured in the same rhyme-scheme. (March 1555). In another manuscript of the sonnet, there is a letter of Michelangelo to Vasari:
"Messer Giorgio, I send you two sonnets: and although they are foolish things, I write (*fo*: 'make') them so that you might see whither my thoughts are tending, and when you are eighty-one years old, as I am, you will believe me. I beg you to give them to messer Giovan Francesco Fattucci who asked me for them. Your Michelagniolo in Roma."

238. The second sonnet sent to Vasari for Fattucci.

239. Although the sheets containing the autograph bear sketches dating back to 1543 and 1545, I would agree with Girardi and Frey who both date the sonnet among the last works. The grave tone of the religiosity surely relates to Michelangelo's final decade, in his 80's.

244. Sonnet written in a "trembling faint hand" according to Girardi.

245. One of the very last sonnets, much rewritten, on a drawing of columns for the library of San Lorenzo.

246. On the back of the final copy of the foregoing.

248. Sonnet for someone who had sent him some gifts, perhaps Vasari. Michelangelo had difficulty accepting gifts. On the back of the autograph is a draft of a letter to Ammanati, and a sketch of the staircase of the Library of San Lorenzo, with two dates: 1 January 1554 and 26 December 1555.

249. This sonnet was written in reply to one sent to Michelangelo by the Archbishop Beccadelli from Ragusa, in February 1556. In his composition Beccadelli after recalling his unhappiness over having been separated from his friend on the occasion of his nunciature in Vienna, laments how much greater still is their present separation but hopes the two friends will meet again in Heaven.

Michelangelo's reply seems somewhat maladroit to me. He is certain he will meet the Bishop in Heaven but prefers to meet him again on earth: his great joy in Heaven will be reunion with his beloved servant Urbino.

250. Probably the first two quattrains of an unfinished sonnet, found together with the following, within a letter from Michelangelo to the Cardinal Ridolfo Pio from Carpi, 1560; the artist was then eighty-five years old.

Michelangelo died in his Roman house at Macel de' Corvi on 18 February, 1564, two weeks before the completion of his eighty-ninth year.

A Note about the Author

Sidney Alexander's translation of Michelangelo's poetry forms the capstone of his celebrated trilogy on the Life and Times of Michelangelo Buonarroti. A widely-recognized scholar in the field of Italian Renaissance studies, Alexander is also the author of three books of poetry, thus bringing into focus especially pertinent qualifications for the translation of Michelangelo's poetry. Alexander's translation and critical edition of Guicciardini's *History of Italy* was awarded the prestigious PEN Award and is the classic work in the field; his *Lions & Foxes*, essays on the Italian Renaissance, is widely used as a text. Mr. Alexander resided in Florence, Italy for thirty years where he was awarded the Grande Medaglia of the Unione Fiorentina for his writings on the Italian Renaissance.

Mr. Alexander is also the author of many books in widely ranging fields: novels, poetry, plays and criticism. His biography of *Chagall* is being published in many foreign languages; his short stories have been included in *Best American Short Stories* and many other anthologies, and he has won the *Maxwell Anderson Award for Dramatic Composition in Verse* on several occasions. He has taught at many Universities, both in Italy and the United States: at Ohio University he held the Morton Chair and was awarded an honorary Ph.D. in 1976; in Italy he has lectured frequently at Stanford and Syracuse Universities.